Nibsy's Gluten-free Recipes

Naomi Lowe

For you, to enjoy.

This book is a celebration of many of the gluten-free experiments that succeeded and were then made many times over, during my time running Reading's first exclusively gluten-free coffee shop.

Having promised a recipe book of many of the Nibsy's 'classics', I sincerely hope you enjoy it and find a few favourites in here.

Idea born in lockdown of 2020.
Sketch by Naomi Lowe.

With love

Hampstead Heath by Cathy Stoker (Naomi's Mum).
This was on display at the coffee shop for many years.

Contents

Beautiful tiles, 26 Cross Street.

And where I spotted a penny (for luck)
months before 1st opening, in 2014.

Introduction

After being diagnosed gluten-intolerant in 2009, I became fed up with the lack of great-tasting gluten-free options that I could eat, especially when visiting coffee shops. I decided to open my own exclusively gluten-free coffee shop in my hometown of Reading and successfully ran it for almost 7 years, learning so much along the way. In Summer 2021 I sold the coffee shop to focus more time on being a mum.

This collection of recipes represents something of a 'bookend' in my gluten-free journey so far and allows me to share with you some of the recipes that made so many local people happy.

At the time of writing this book, my son Bradley was watching Disney's Ratatouille on repeat, and the message in the story? "Anyone can cook". And that's it. I've never written a book and eight years ago I could barely bake, but it's all about having a good recipe that's clear to follow and applied with care and attention, with the intention to spread love and joy. With practice confidence grows.

About Me

I'm Naomi Lowe and nicknamed "Nibsylove" by my mum from an early age – hence Nibsy. I live in Reading with my husband Jon and my two gorgeous young boys, Bradley and Leonard.

I grew up in a large and loving family. Despite not being academically minded, my mum and dad always believed in my abilities. My brothers and I were all brought up vegetarian.

I have such fond memories of mum cooking for us, especially during our time in the South West of France where I spent five years of my childhood. We lived in an old farmhouse in a tiny village called Cazeneuve-Montaut, overlooked by the Pyrenees and were always well fed on gorgeous home-cooked meals.

The dream of having a little happy place for people to come to had always been simmering in the background from a young age. As a child and teenager, I'd sometimes turn our kitchen and living room into a little café for my family. I'd create menus and "invite" my mum, dad and brothers to choose their order whilst I'd wander off into the kitchen and improvise – for me, the fun was just as much about the "feeling" as it was the homecooked food.

In my early-twenties I had an "out of the blue" anaphylactic reaction to an apple in the centre of London. The speed at which the Ambulance arrived and peeled me off the pavement that day probably saved my life.

Over the next few years, I started to feel more and more unwell and couldn't work out what was causing it. My doctor recommended I go on a gluten-free diet for a week to see if I noticed any change. I did and even after just a week I felt so much better – I couldn't believe that gluten had been the culprit. Finding this out was the biggest relief; I'd finally found a solution to being back to 'me' again.

At the time of switching to a strictly gluten-free diet, I was working at an investment company in Henley-on-Thames and it was there that I met my husband, Jon. As time went on, my mind was wondering if I could take a change of direction and finally create my little (exclusively gluten-free) happy place. Nowhere near me was catering for people like us and I desperately wanted to fill what I saw as a huge gap in the coffee shop sector when it came to gluten-free options. So many of us were missing out on one of life's small but important pleasures; gorgeous homemade cakes alongside a favourite hot drink.

I would draw mind maps, with doodles and visions of what the coffee shop would look like. Through times of self-doubt I'd screw them up and throw them in the bin only to fish them out a few days later and iron away the creases. When Jon realised how serious I was becoming about wanting to make it happen, he encouraged me to go for it. In spring 2013 I had my first son, Bradley, and I spent a great deal of that magical maternity time developing a plan of action. I had virtually no baking experience, but my mum and I would experiment with recipes. I didn't even drink coffee at the time, and here I was, dreaming of opening a coffee shop!

I was well aware that I'd need to learn fast. My gut told me "it will work" and I'd have to enjoy the experience, recruit and employ great people, learn from others, be resourceful and adapt. I'd often have to remind myself of the '80/20 rule'. But the goal never changed and was always: Create somewhere special, with great service and humble, gluten-free food. Plus, I'd decided that it was vital that the coffee shop was entirely gluten-free. Of course, I realised this decision would potentially limit the appeal to a minority of people; There was, and still is, a bit of a stigma with gluten-free food and how it compares to "normal" versions of the same bakes.

But it had to be that or nothing and I wanted to do it properly. The journey of going from the idea to trading was pretty bonkers in terms of how much had to be done. There were tons of obstacles I had to overcome, I had borrowed an awful lot of money, walked away from a safe job that I enjoyed - and I had a toddler.

Nibsy's opened on 2nd September 2014 and soon turned into a little hub where people would come and enjoy some downtime, a treat, a catch up with friends and a bit of 'sunshine', even on a cold day. It was a big privilege for the team and I to have such a diverse and lovely customer base that really appreciated what we all did.

At the heart of the business was a passion for making really great gluten-free treats, without compromise. Of course, this meant trials and errors and just going with it and having a great team of people. Creating and running a business requires discipline, commitment and passion as well as juggling big overheads and I loved the challenge.

The coffee shop went from strength to strength and was enjoyed not just by those with a gluten intolerance or coeliac disease, but those who are lucky enough to be totally indifferent to the fact everything was gluten-free. People enjoyed the food because it was good.

In early 2020 COVID19 headed our way. It was then, while the business was temporarily closed, that the idea of writing this book and sharing the recipes started. Jon would be in charge of the kids while I got the laptop out on the kitchen table and started collating loads of the Nibsy's 'staples' that had been adored over the years – with the aim of keeping the spirit of that happy place alive, until we could re-open. The recipe book was parked for a while, but not forgotten.

By early 2021, the coffee shop was riding the waves of change really well, thanks to constantly adapting around the various restrictions and opportunities. However, running the business and balancing motherhood was taking its toll and I made the very difficult decision to sell the coffee shop so I could have more quality time with my boys and cherish them, while they are still young.

The new owners, Richard and Helen, gave the coffee shop a new name (as I couldn't leave the name behind) but most importantly, they kept it entirely gluten-free (www. Yaylo.co) along with many of the recipes some of you grew to love. And they understood that I would eventually be sharing these with you. If you're local to Reading, please continue to support them.

Despite having walked away from the dream that I'd made into a reality, I'm incredibly proud of what was achieved and that my hometown still has somewhere dedicated to all of us who can't eat gluten.

I am so immensely grateful for all the support from so many of you including staff, suppliers and of course the best customers I could have ever wished for. I have met some really wonderful people.

Getting this book over the line has been a very personal process and it comes from the heart. I hope you find the recipes easy to follow and that the results bring you joy, many times over.

Happy Baking ☺

Naomi x

"Walking home". By Naomi Lowe

About Gluten

The chances are, if you're reading this book you know about how important the absence of gluten is for anyone needing to have a gluten-free diet.

The internet is full of information and is a great place to find out the answers to any questions you have. Two great sources for up to date information are Coeliac UK who are a charity www.coeliac.org.uk as well as the NHS website www.nhs.uk.

Here is some key information:

What is gluten?

Definition of gluten (from Latin gluten, "glue")

– Gluten is a protein composite found in wheat and related grains, including barley and rye and is responsible for the elastic texture of dough.

Wheat-free is not the same as "gluten-free". Gluten may still be present in products that are labeled wheat-free, as gluten is also present in barley, rye or oats (unless the oats are specifically labelled as gluten-free).

What does "gluten-free" mean?

It simply means excluding all food containing "gluten" from your diet.

The real impact of this means not being able to eat some of the best comfort foods, processed foods and every-day staples. And buying the gluten-free versions often costs more.

Who should eat a gluten-free diet?

Anyone who's been diagnosed with coeliac disease or has a gluten sensitivity.

A gluten-free diet is also popular among people who haven't been diagnosed with a gluten-related medical condition. The claimed benefits of the diet are improved health, weight loss and increased energy, but more research is needed.

What is Coeliac Disease?

Coeliac disease is an autoimmune condition. This is where the immune system (the body's defense against infection) mistakenly attacks the healthy tissue.

With coeliac disease, the immune system mistakes substances found inside gluten as a threat to the body and attacks them.

This damages the surface of the small bowel (intestines), disrupting the body's ability to take in nutrients from food. The small intestine is lined with tiny hairlike projections called villi, which absorb vitamins, minerals and other nutrients from the food we eat. Coeliac disease damages the villi, leaving the body unable to absorb nutrients necessary for health and growth.

Therefore the only cure for coeliac disease is to have a strictly gluten-free diet. Once someone with coeliac disease switches to an entirely gluten-free diet, their small intestine will start to repair itself and absorb nutrients once again.

What is gluten sensitivity/intolerance?

The symptoms of gluten sensitivity are usually similar to those of undiagnosed coeliac disease, but the two conditions are different. It is not clear if the immune system is affected in the same way as it is with coeliac disease.

What are the symptoms?

The symptoms of coeliac disease and/or gluten sensitivity vary from person to person and can sometimes seem unrelated, here are a few examples:

· Stomach pain or bloating, gas and/or cramps
· Nausea and or Vomiting
· Constipation or Diarrhea
· Anemia
· Depression and unexplained mood swings
· Unintentional weight loss or weight gain
· Joint pain
· Tiredness (fatigue) as a result of not getting enough nutrients from food (malnutrition)
· Itchy skin and other skin conditions
· Headaches
· Slow infant and child growth and possible delayed puberty

Can you become coeliac or sensitive to gluten?

Yes, it can develop at any age. Some people have symptoms of this condition earlier in life, while others don't have signs until they're older.

When it comes to coeliac disease, the exact cause of this autoimmune disorder is unknown. One theory is that some microorganisms (such as bacteria or viruses) or drugs may trigger changes that confuse the immune system.

How to diagnose it?

Doctors can do a test to determine if there are elevated levels of antibodies to gluten in the blood. For positive results, sometimes a biopsy of the small intestine is necessary to determine if any damage has been done. There are also tests online.

Living gluten-free

If you've recently had to make the switch to a gluten-free diet or are cooking for someone else, it can feel a bit daunting at first.

Finding gluten-free products

· Read labels and allergy panels
· Look out for any warnings that state 'may contain traces of gluten....'
· The law requires that any packaged product must state clearly if it contains a known allergen, ie gluten.

Eating out and cooking at home

This can be challenging, depending on venues. There's the risk of cross contamination to worry about, usually a smaller menu choice too. And when the food arrives, it's normal to want to check, check and double check with the waiter that the plate of food doesn't contain gluten.

When it comes to cooking at home it's important to reduce the chances of cross contamination as much as possible by being aware of doing the following:

- Thoroughly clean work surfaces
- Use clean tea towels
- Use a separate toaster and chopping boards
- Make sure any utensils, bowls and equipment are completely clean before use
- Prepare the gluten-free food separately to anything else
- Have a dedicated area if possible
- Store gluten-free products in separate containers, away from any gluten-containing products

Lots of it is common sense and being aware of any risk factors and taking great care. So if you're unsure of anything, definitely use other books or websites for more information.

Savoury Recipes

Cheesy Balls

The official name for these is 'Pao de queijo' which means cheesy bread. They are a typical Brazilian breakfast item, usually enjoyed with a black coffee. I was introduced to these by Céline Lee, owner of Cocolico pâtisserie who previously worked as baker at the coffee shop. She discovered them when she worked in a Brazilian restaurant in Paris and fell in love with the cheesy texture. When you try these, you'll see exactly why they are incredibly more-ish and are great for parties, BBQs, or on the side with a salad or olives.

 12 Balls   **20 minutes**   **20-30 minutes at 165°C**

Ingredients

- 400g tapioca starch
- 100g potato starch
- 10g salt
- 200ml **milk**
- 70ml sunflower oil
- 300g grated mature cheddar (**milk**)
- 4 small **eggs**

Optional – top with cumin seeds, cracked salt, extra cheese

Equipment

Scales

Measuring jug

Small saucepan

Large bowl

Grater

Whisk

Parchment paper

Baking tray

Method

1. Pre-heat the oven to 165°C/325°F/gas mark 3 and line a large baking tray with parchment paper.

2. In a large bowl mix the tapioca, potato starch and salt. In small pan, bring the milk and oil to a boil, then quickly pour it into the dry ingredients and mix with a wooden spoon or a spatula (not your hands initially, as the liquids will be too hot). Once the mixture is cool enough to touch, mix it using your hands. The texture will look and feel strange and chunky but this is normal.

3. Add the grated cheese and mix it all in, again using your hands. And finally crack the eggs into the mixture and using your hands, thoroughly mixing it until everything is nice and evenly distributed. The batter is now ready to be rolled into balls, which is a little challenging as you'll find that the dough is really sticky and will cling to your hands! So to help, you may need to squeeze a small amount of oil in your hands and then shape the balls (it helps if you have someone who can do this for you!).

4. To get 12 balls from this recipe, each raw dough ball should weigh about 90g each but you can make them any size you want and adjust the cooking time accordingly.

5. Place the balls on the lined baking tray, leaving a 5cm gap between each ball so they have room to expand a little in the oven. Sprinkle them with a dash of cracked salt, a dash of cumin seeds and a little extra cheese, if you wish, and bake them in the oven for 20-30 minutes until golden. Enjoy them warm.

6. Eat within 2 days. Store them in an air-tight container and warm them up for about 30 seconds in the microwave.

Top Tips

Choose the smallest eggs, otherwise the texture will be too sticky. The dough will look strange and feel odd and very sticky; and you may think you've done something wrong, but keep going with it and just make sure you get your hands stuck in. Even though it's a super sticky dough, make sure to squelch the ingredients really well together before forming them into balls.

Coleslaw

I know it might seem a bit odd to include coleslaw, but I've made lots of it over the years and friends and family always say how nice it is. A quality portion of homemade coleslaw goes well on the side of many main meals and helps give starchy foods a lift.

I was first shown how to make this when I was about 15 years old and working my first regular job as a waitress at the Bottle and Glass pub in Binfield Heath village. It was run by Anne and Mike Robinson at the time and was a stunning little authentic country pub which they ran brilliantly. I have many happy memories of working there and it helped fund my teenage social life (oh to be young again!). Anne was my first "boss" and we had a good bond. One of the first things she showed me was how to make the coleslaw and here's how...

 4–6 Portions   **10 minutes**   **No**

Ingredients

- 190g white cabbage (you can use red too, but I think white tastes nicer)
- 190g carrots, peeled and grated
- 100g onions (white or red) finely chopped into strips
- Salt and pepper
- 120g full fat Hellmann's mayonnaise (**eggs**)

Equipment

Scales   Large bowl   Grater

Sharp knife   Peeler

Method

1. Depending on how much coleslaw you want to make, increase or decrease the ingredients proportionately.

2. Starting with the cabbage, tear away any of the not so pretty outer bits and cut the desired amount into ½ cm (0.2") strips. Then cut these long slim strips into halves and avoid using the hard central bit of the cabbage. Place the strips into a bowl and add the peeled and grated carrots along with the finely cut white onions.

3. Toss everything around so that it's well mixed and add loads of salt and pepper. I recommend you use quality cracked salt instead of standard cooking salt – it's so much nicer. Same goes for pepper. Mix the seasoning into the vegetables, tossing everything around again.

4. Add the mayonnaise and use two dessertspoons to mix it all up until you have a coleslaw that is neither too wet nor too sparing of mayonnaise. I usually season it again at this point but I'd recommend you taste it before seeing if this is needed.

5. Store airtight in the fridge, for 3 to 4 days.

Top Tips

Just follow the recipe and get the seasoning right. Use Hellmann's mayonnaise unless you've found a brand that you really like. To make this vegan, just use a vegan mayo instead.

Allergens in bold

Lemon and mustard
dressing

Lemon & Mustard Dressing

Back in 2014 when Harriet and Illaria worked together in the kitchen at the coffee shop, they would make this really easy dressing for us to use on garnishes to accompany the quiche and we continued to use keep the dressing the same throughout the years. It's a great recipe because it's light and versatile so it goes really well with many types of salads.

 550ml approx (1 Pint)
halve the recipe if you want less

 10 minutes

 No

Ingredients

- 160ml extra virgin olive oil
- 125ml pre-bought lemon juice (**sulphates**) or use freshly squeezed juice from lemons
- 250ml sunflower oil
- ½ x tablespoon of salt
- ½ x tablespoon of gluten-free English or Dijon **mustard**
- 40g light brown sugar
- 2 x tablespoon of dry thyme, wrapped and secured in a J-cloth with a clip

Equipment

Scales

Measuring jug

J-cloth & Clip

Large bowl

Measuring spoons

Whisk

Method

1. Simply weigh all the ingredients into a large bowl, apart from the thyme, and whisk them all together.

2. Put the thyme in the centre of a J-cloth and tie the cloth tightly with an elastic band or clip so that no herbs can escape. Once secure, submerge this into the dressing allowing it to absorb into the oils and, ideally, keep it in there for the life of the dressing.

3. Shake or stir the dressing before each use. The dressing will last at least a month in the fridge, in an air-tight container.

Allergens in bold

Mum's Pasta Sauce
Versatile base sauce for many dishes

The oldest recipe in the book and my absolute favourite. My mum has made this throughout my childhood and beyond. It's one of best base sauces I have ever tasted and it's a family favourite. It's basically an onion-based sauce, slow cooked with layers of simple flavours added, along with tomato and herbs.

This sauce can be used as a base for so many dishes, from pasta, chilli, lasagne, pizza topping, dipping sauce for cheese and biscuits, tortilla chips, and even in quiches. You will probably want to add some roasted vegetables to it once it's made as this helps it go even further.

It's quite an oily sauce but the oils are full of flavour. The sauce will make your house smell of onions, unless you have a good extractor fan! I remember having to make a lot of it shortly after my second son, Leonard, was born, and all his new baby clothes that were washed and drying smelt of onions for days! I was in such a low place at that time, but a happy memory is of sitting at the kitchen table with my dad, while we battled our way through cutting many, many onions as we were making large batches, sipping on wine, while he watched University Challenge (his Monday night ritual). And I'd be lucky to get one question right!

Here's an example of the sauce used as a dip and over gluten-free pasta, toppped with cheese.

1 large pan's worth
of about 2.2kg worth of sauce

 **20 minutes**
(Cutting the onions)

 1.5 to 2 hours

 Yes

Ingredients

- 375ml sunflower oil
- 2kg white onions, peeled and finely chopped
- 1 bulb of garlic, peeled and pressed/crushed
- Lots of salt and cracked black pepper
- 2 x tablespoons of demerara sugar
- 150ml balsamic vinegar
- 3 x tablespoons of dried Italian mixed herbs
- 200g tomato purée
- 1 x tablespoon of chilli oil
- ½ x teaspoon chilli flakes
- 2 x tablespoons sweet chilli sauce (optional)
- 400g tinned, chopped tomatoes

Equipment

Scales

Chopping knife

Large saucepan

Garlic crusher

Measuring jug

Mixing spoon

Measuring spoons

Method

1. I know it might seem like a lot of onions, but they are relatively cheap and so you might as well get a large batch of sauce for your efforts. Once the onions have been chopped the hard work is done. The main thing with this recipe is to let everything cook slowly and layer the ingredients bit by bit. The total cooking time for the quantity here should be around 1 hour 30 minutes to 2 hours and the last ingredient (the chopped tomatoes) must not go in until all other ingredients have been cooking for at least 1hour and 15 minutes. This ensures there's loads of depth of flavour having had plenty of time to intensify first.

2. Simply follow the recipe in this order and use the times as a guide to help you do the layering at the recommended pace to achieve the most beautifully rich sauce!

3. Peel, weigh and chop the onions into chunks: You need them to be roughly chopped but not super fine. The perfect size for each strip of onion is approximately ½cm wide and 3cm long.

4. Put the sunflower oil in a large pan on a medium heat and once hot, add the onions and stir in the crushed garlic. Add 2 teaspoon of salt and lots of cracked pepper. Leave them to slowly cook on a medium heat for 30 minutes stirring regularly to make sure the onions are evenly cooked throughout, supple and slightly caramelised in colour.

5. After 30 minutes is up, add 2 tablespoons sugar to the onions, to help make them even more caramelised. Stir regularly for a further 20 minutes and turn the heat down to low, stirring regularly to prevent the onions from burning on the bottom of the pan.

6. Add the balsamic vinegar and another half teaspoon of salt and some more cracked pepper. Stir and cook for another 10 minutes.

7. Mix in the dried herbs and cook for another 5 minutes.

8. Add the tomato purée and mix it in well and turn the hob back to a medium heat and allow to cook gently for another 15 minutes.

9. Add the chili oil and chili flakes (or you can omit these if you don't want the tiny kick these will bring) and cook for another 5 minutes. If you want to add 2 tablespoons of chili sauce, you can add this in now as well.

10. Finally add the tinned tomatoes and cook for a further 10mins, stirring well, and once the sauce is gently bubbling taste it to check if the seasoning is OK.

11. This step is optional - transfer the sauce to an oven-proof glass dish and pop it in the oven on a low heat, until the top of the sauce looks a little deeper in colour. This will take up to half-an-hour.

12. You can use the sauce straight away or decant into jars or food storage boxes once cooled. To make the sauce go further, add roasted or fried vegetables of your choice. Mushrooms work especially well with it.

13. Keep airtight in the fridge or freezer. It will last 2 weeks in the fridge, thanks to the vinegar.

Top Tips

Don't rush it. The longer you are prepared to take to layer the ingredients the better the sauce will taste.

Pizza

Yes! A vegan pizza base and it's up to you what sort of cheese and toppings you put on top! This is a fairly thick pizza base with some bounce to it. Of course it depends how thinly you decide to spread the pizza dough and the size of your pizza tray but it's versatile and this recipe is based on making two large pizzas.

This was an instant hit when Céline, who previously worked as a baker at the coffee shop, said she had a great pizza dough recipe to share. This recipe is based on using a gluten-free bread flour mix by Doves Farm but I am sure that any gluten-free bread flour mix will work, however I have not tried making it using a standard gluten-free flour such as plain or self-raising and would recommend you stick with a gluten-free bread flour.

Making homemade pizza is a fun way to get the little ones to eat vegetables and get involved with the decorating of the pizza (is that even the right term?!!). You'll just need to make sure you've made the dough at least 6 hours before cooking it as it needs time to rise. Or you can even make it the day before and leave it in the fridge overnight, ready for the next day.

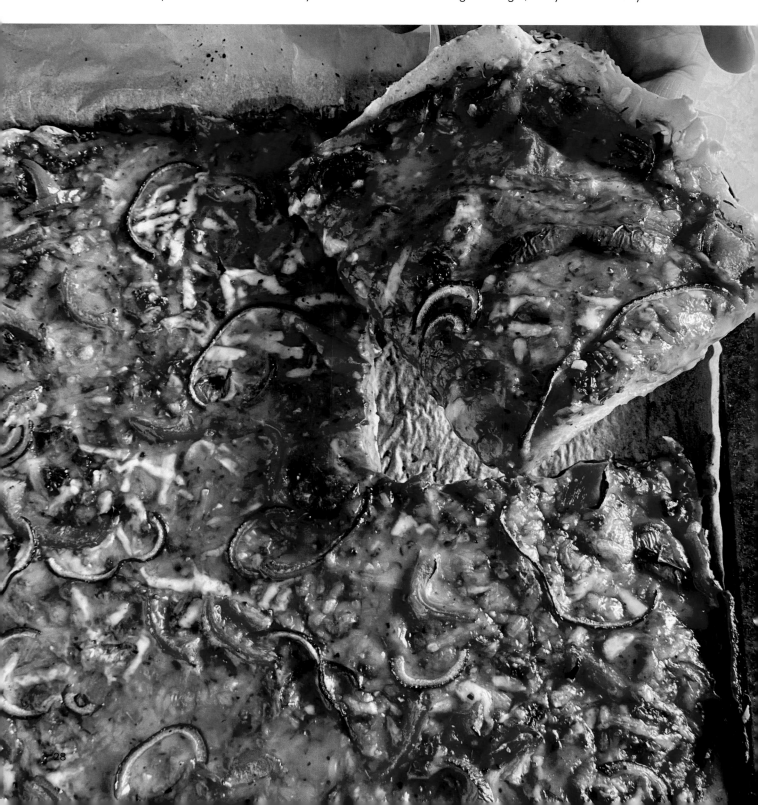

2 medium-sized oven trays or one really large one.
If using a tray measuring 30cm (12") x 20cm (8") you'll make two pizzas

15 minutes plus time to allow dough to rise overnight

25+mins at 180°C

No

Ingredients

Pizza dough

- 60g aquafaba water (that's the water from a can of chickpeas)
- 65ml extra virgin olive oil
- 1 x teaspoon balsamic vinegar
- 400ml **soya** milk
- 1.5 x tablespoon caster sugar
- 1 x teaspoon salt
- 500g gluten-free white bread flour
- 2 x teaspoon gluten-free quick yeast

Toppings

- 350g passata (or you can use some of the Pasta sauce (page 27)
- Generous dose of salt and pepper
- Dried oregano or fresh basil
- Dried garlic powder (optional)
- 150g **cheese** (vegan or dairy)

  Followed by toppings such as:

  Mixed olives, red onion, peppers, mushrooms, tomato, sweetcorn, chilli oil etc

Equipment

Baking tray · Parchment paper · Scales

Measuring jug · Large bowl · Measuring spoons

Spatula · Grater · Clean tea towel

Hand whisk or Electric whisk

Method

1. Simply weigh all the liquid ingredients in the pizza dough ingredients list along with the salt and sugar into a large bowl or cake mixer. Then add the gluten-free bread flour so that it covers everything, then add the yeast on top.

2. Using either a cake mixer, or hand-held electric whisk, attach the hook accessory and spin everything together at medium-high speed for a few minutes until you're happy that any lumps have been taken care of and the dough is looking consistent throughout.

3. Keep the mixture in the same bowl (as long as there is good clearance between the dough and the top of the bowl, to allow room for the dough to rise). Cover with a clean and damp tea-towel and let it sit overnight in the fridge to develop, or if you make it 6 hours before needing to use it, you can leave it covered in a warm spot.

4. The next day or 6 hours later, pre-heat the oven to 180°C/350°F/gas mark 4 and line your baking tray(s) with parchment paper. Spread the dough across the tray(s). I have found that the easiest way to spread the dough is with the back of a dessertspoon, confidently spreading it to the corners and evenly throughout – very satisfying once you've got the knack!

5. Spread the tomato passata/sauce over the dough, season with lots of salt, pepper and fresh basil and/or dried oregano – add some garlic powder, if you wish, or a finely chop a couple of fresh garlic cloves. Add as much or as little of the cheese (vegan or non-vegan) as you want, followed by your choice of toppings, and some extra herbs and seasoning.

6. The baking time will depend on the thickness of the base, the tray size you've used as well as how generous you've been with the cheese and toppings. I would expect it to bake for at least 20 minutes or more. Once ready, the edges of the pizza should be golden with a slight crunch.

7. Store any leftover pizza in the fridge for up to 3 days or freeze.

Top Tips

You have to plan in advance with this because the dough needs to develop and this takes about 5-6 hours. Typically, it's best to simply leave the dough in the fridge overnight, in a large bowl that allows room for the growth. Or, if you make it earlier enough in the morning and leave it somewhere naturally warm, it will rise enough to be used after 5 to 6 hours.

Allergens in bold

Introduction to Quiches

Here's your guide to gluten-free quiches that taste great thanks to good gluten-free pastry and a generous filling. These two things are hard to come by when buying shop-bought gluten-free quiches.

The quiches were always so popular at the coffee shop; they'd always vary in flavour, using whatever vegetables were available, and I have made so many combinations to date I couldn't list them all! But our customers loved them.

Quiches are such a British classic and are pretty versatile. Although they do take some effort to make when making the pastry - but all the best things take a little time. They can be enjoyed hot, cold, with salad, or vegetables, chips, or just on their own! And they are a great savoury option when catering for lots of people as they can be made in advance and are easy to serve.

Over the next few pages you'll find various flavour combinations to try. You can of course improvise. When cooking savoury things it's quite easy to be spontaneous. So if you see a vegetable you'd like to swap for something else then go for it.

Before you start

Please take the time to read these useful tips, they will help a lot and are worth the time!

Pastry

First thing is to have a great batch of blind-baked, golden pastry. So for the perfect gluten-free pastry, head over to that section first (page 101).

Seasoning

As with almost all savoury food, seasoning is key. So when preparing the vegetables, be sure to season them properly. And once the whole mixture is ready to go into the pastry case, if you are brave enough, dip your finger in the raw mixture and taste it to double check the seasoning is right and adjust it if it isn't.

Choosing your vegetables

The recipes here are just ideas so please mix them up if you want. I always recommend using fresh herbs to bring the quiche flavour alive. You can also add spices such as curry powder, turmeric, cumin seeds etc, all of which give the quiche a new dimension. Just be sure that the flavours and vegetables you're choosing to put in the quiche complement the vegetables. Also think about what's in season, and there's nothing wrong with using frozen vegetables too.

Filling the pastry case with the filling

Before filling the pastry case (which needs to be blind-baked first), check for any cracks; they are normal and as long as you have a sheet of parchment paper lining the tin under the pastry, then any quiche mixture will stay within the tin, albeit that a bit may seep under the pastry a little. Any cracks on the outer rim of the pastry can be easily repaired using small torn-off pieces of parchment paper to create little barriers as you see fit.

It's good to be generous with the filling to achieve a chunky quiche full to the brim whilst also not allowing any spillage over the top and down the sides. So fill your case to just a smidge below the line of where the pastry ends.

Baking the quiche

Cooking the quiches is best at a low temperature of between 165°c to 170°c/325F/gas mark 3. This allows the quiche to cook in the middle whilst not overdoing the top and keeping the colours alive. It makes for a much prettier result too.

Pop it in the oven for 25 minutes and check to see if it needs turning 180 degrees and then bake it for up to another 25 minutes. The total cooking time will depend on the oven and how full the quiche is. When you think it's ready to come out be sure to check that the middle looks cooked and only has a very subtle "wobble".

Looking after your quiche.

Once cooked, the quiche is delicate when warm so if eating it straight away, handle it with care when taking it out the tin. If you're saving it for later or another day, cover it with clingfilm once it's cooled down and store it in the fridge or freezer.

The quiche can be reheated in the oven but avoid the microwave as it will make the pastry less flakey. Defrosting the quiche takes a few hours and if kept in the fridge, will last about 4 days.

Asparagus, Leek & Red Pepper Quiche

It's best to do this when the asparagus is in season, and for ease you can use roasted red peppers straight from a jar. This is delicious warmed up or served cold. Once cooked, it smells incredible. There was a time when making quiches was a regular weekly routine at the coffee shop and during the various lockdown and closures I'd miss making them and this is one I made at home and I hope you'll enjoy making it too.

 1 x 25cm (10") flan dish   **45 minutes**   **40-50 minutes at 165°C**   **Yes**

Ingredients

Pastry

This will produce 1 x batch of pastry to fill a 25cm (10") flan dish.

- 235g Doves Farm gluten-free plain flour
- 125g butter (frozen into chunks) (**milk**) or dairy-free alternative
- 1 x teaspoon salt
- 1 medium **egg**
- 2 x tablespoon ice cold water (or 1 tablespoon if using dairy-free 'butter')

Quiche Filling

This will fill 1 quiche using a 10" inch / 25cm baking dish.

Base flavours:

- 250g chopped leeks
- 3 x tablespoons sunflower or olive oil
- 3 garlic cloves, crushed
- 125g asparagus
- 10g butter (**milk**)
- 160g extra mature Cheddar cheese (**milk**)
- 2 x teaspoon dried thyme
- 10g fresh chives, chopped
- 175g finely sliced red pepper from a jar, drained (or fresh – see method)
- Salt and pepper

Quiche Custard

- 90ml **milk**
- 90ml double cream (**milk**)
- 3 medium **eggs**
- 1 x teaspoon salt
- Lots of cracked black pepper

Method

1. To avoid repetition for each of the quiche's flavours, please read the introduction section to quiches for tips to help create a great quiche!

2. Have your pastry ready and blind baked, in your chosen baking tin and make sure it's also lined with parchment paper. (See pastry recipe on page 101).

3. This quiche filing recipe is based on filling a 10 inch / 25cm quiche dish. Pre-heat the oven to 165°C/325°F/gas mark 3.

4. Wash the leeks and finely chop them. Fry them on a medium heat, with 3 tablespoons of sunflower oil and add the peeled, crushed garlic. Season and cook until they are wilted, soft and have some colour. This will take at least 15 minutes.

5. In a separate pan, gently fry the asparagus with a bit of sunflower oil and 10g butter and a little seasoning until they are soft whilst still holding their 'body'.

6. Once the leeks and asparagus are cooked, put them together in a large bowl. Add the grated Cheddar cheese, fresh chives and 2 x teaspoon dried thyme.

7. Add 175g of drained red peppers from a jar and finely slice them. If using fresh peppers, simply fry them until soft on a medium heat then add to them to the bowl.

8. Now for the quiche custard; put the milk, double cream and eggs together in a jug or bowl, season with 1 x teaspoon salt and lots of cracked black pepper, and mix. Then pour this into the bowl with all the vegetables and cheese and give everything a good stir.

9. Carefully spoon the mixture into the pastry case and pop it in the oven for 25 minutes. After 25 minutes, check to see if it needs turning and bake it for another 15 to 25 minutes depending on how deep your quiche is. When it's ready it shouldn't wobble but we don't want it overcooked either, so just see what you think and go with your gut feeling.

10. Allow the quiche to cool a little before taking it out of the tin and serving. This flavour is especially nice cold, too.

11. Store airtight in the fridge for up to 4 days or freeze. To re-heat, use the oven.

Equipment (Quiche filling only, for pastry see page 101)

Large bowl   2x frying pans   Grater   Scales   Measuring jug   Sharp knife

Allergens in bold

Butternut Squash & Goat's Cheese Quiche

A classic combination with sweet potato, Cheddar, fresh basil and red onions. This one is so good in the autumn and winter and goes really well with a side salad drizzled with balsamic glaze.

 1 25cm (10") flan dish   **1 hour**   **50 minutes at 165°C**   **Yes**

Ingredients

Pastry

This will produce 1 x batch of pastry to fill a 25cm (10") flan dish.

- 235g Doves Farm gluten-free plain flour
- 125g butter (frozen into chunks) (**milk**) or dairy-free alternative
- 1 x teaspoon salt
- 1 medium **egg**
- 2 x tablespoon ice cold water (or 1 tablespoon if using dairy-free 'butter')

Filling

This will fill 1 quiche using a 25cm (10") flan dish.

- 400g butternut squash
- 200g sweet potato
- 2 small red onions
- 2 x tablespoon sunflower oil
- 1 x teaspoon balsamic vinegar
- 150g goat's **cheese**
- 100g grated mature Cheddar **cheese** (**milk**)
- 1 handful of freshly chopped basil

Quiche Custard

- 90ml **milk**
- 90ml double **cream**
- 4 medium **eggs**
- 1 x teaspoon salt
- Lots of cracked black pepper

Method

It starts with great pastry; see page 101 for all the information. If you're making the pastry for the first time, I promise that the more you do it, the easier it will become.

1. It's also a good idea to read the "Introduction to quiches", page 31 first, for tips before you continue.

2. Once the pastry is blind baked and ready, and lined with parchment paper under the pastry, put it to one side.

3. Pre-heat the oven to 165°C/325°F/gas mark 3. Peel and chop 400g of butternut squash into small chunks. Also peel and chop 200g worth of sweet potato, making sure the chunks are a bit bigger than the butternut squash chunks and place them in a large bowl with a dash of sunflower oil, salt and pepper. Mix and transfer to a large baking tray lined with parchment paper. Or you can cook these root vegetables on separate baking trays. Roast them until they are soft but not mushy. The cooking time will entirely depend on how big or small the chunks are, but allow about 30 minutes.

4. While the butternut squash is roasting, peel and chop the red onions and fry them in a pan with 2 x tablespoons sunflower oil, optional crushed garlic, salt and pepper. Once they are half-cooked, add a teaspoon balsamic vinegar and cook until they are golden. Allow 10 to 15 minutes, stirring regularly.

5. Chop the goat's cheese into chunks, and add to a large bowl, along with the grated Cheddar and chopped basil. Once the onions and the roasted vegetables are ready, add them to the bowl and mix everything.

6. For the custard, weigh the milk and double cream into a separate bowl or jug and add the eggs and seasoning. Mix together and then pour this into the bowl with all the other ingredients. Check the seasoning and adjust.

7. Carefully fill the pastry case with the mixture and cook it in the oven at 165C/17C. After 25 minutes, check to see if it needs turning and bake it for another 10-25 minutes. Cooking times will vary so keep an eye on it towards the end. Once ready, allow it to cool a little before taking it out of the tin.

8. Store airtight in the fridge for up to 4 days or freeze. To re-heat, use the oven.

Equipment (Quiche filling only, for pastry see page 101)

Scales	Measuring jug	Sharp knife	Parchment paper
Whisk	Large bowl	Baking tray	Grater

Mediterranean Flavours Quiche

This flavour combination is one of my favourites and it's partly because it includes a quick version of my mum's pasta sauce (full recipe on page 27) to give it depth. If you've already got round to making the sauce you'll know how good and versatile it is and a little of it in the quiche gives it such a boost in flavour. But the sauce takes a few hours to make so there is an alternative way of doing it if that works better for you and the quiche will still taste great!

1 x 25cm (10") flan dish **45 minutes** **50 minutes at 165°C** **Yes**

Ingredients

Pastry

This will produce 1 x batch of pastry to fill a 25cm (10") flan dish.

- 235g Doves Farm gluten-free plain flour
- 125g butter (frozen into chunks) (**milk**) or dairy-free alternative
- 1 x teaspoon salt
- 1 medium **egg**
- 2 x tablespoon ice cold water (or 1 tablespoon if using dairy-free 'butter')

Filling

This will fill 1 quiche using a 25cm (10") baking dish.

Base flavours

- 130g Mum's pasta sauce, page 27

  or

  Make a quick version with the following:

- 4 medium sized red or white onions
- 4 cloves of crushed garlic
- 4x tablespoon sunflower oil
- 1 x teaspoon brown sugar
- 1 x teaspoon mixed dried herbs
- 2 x teaspoon balsamic vinegar
- Half a tube of concentrated tomato purée

Main Flavours

- 1 teaspoon mixed herbs
- 225g courgette
- 75g yellow pepper
- 200g mushrooms
- 2 x cloves of garlic
- 140g mature Cheddar cheese, grated (**milk**)
- 0.5 teaspoon ground turmeric

Quiche Custard

- 90ml **milk**
- 90ml double cream (**milk**)
- 4 medium **eggs**
- 1 x teaspoon salt
- Lots of cracked black pepper

Method

1. A great quiche starts with great pastry; see page 101 for all the information. If you're making the pastry for the first time, I promise that the more you do it, the easier it will become (as with most things!).

2. It's a good idea to read the "Introduction to quiches", page 31 first, for tips before you continue.

3. Make the filling.

   A) You'll either need 130g of the pasta sauce (found on page 27) which you just need to park to one side for now.

   B) Or follow these steps to create a quick version of the sauce: Finely chop 4 onions and crush 4 cloves of garlic and fry them in a pan on a medium heat, along with 4 tablespoons of sunflower oil. Cook the onions with the garlic until soft, then add a teaspoon of brown sugar to help caramelise and sweeten up the onions and cook for another 10 minutes. Add the herbs and mix them in, then add 2 x teaspoon balsamic vinegar and cook for another 5 minutes on a slow heat, stirring regularly. Finally add the half tube of concentrated tomato purée and gently cook for a further 5 minutes. Once this is ready, park it to one side and read on.

4. Once the above is sorted, preheat the oven to 165C°C/325°F/gas mark 3. Chop the courgette and yellow pepper and gently fry together in a pan with plenty of seasoning. In another pan, chop the mushrooms and add 2 cloves of garlic and cook until soft and colourful, adding a teaspoon of mixed dried herbs. Once the vegetables are cooked, put them all in a large bowl, along with the onion & tomato sauce and the grated Cheddar. Add the ground turmeric. Give it a good stir.

5. For the quiche custard, put the milk, double cream and eggs together in a jug or bowl, season with 1 x teaspoon salt and lots of cracked black pepper and mix. Then pour this into the bowl with all the vegetables and cheese and stir well.

6. Once you've checked the seasoning (only if you can bear it, as this requires tasting raw egg) and are happy with it, gently spoon the mixture into the pastry case.

7. Pop it in the oven for 25 minutes. After 25 minutes, check to see if it needs turning and bake it for another 15-25 minutes. When it's ready it shouldn't wobble but we don't want it overcooked either, so just see what you think and go with your gut feeling. Once ready, allow to cool slightly before taking it out of the tin and enjoy straight away, or enjoy later.

8. Store airtight in the fridge for up to 4 days or freeze. To re-heat, use the oven on a medium setting.

Equipment (Quiche filling only, for pastry see page 101)

Scales   Measuring jug   Sharp knife

Grater   Frying pan   Whisk

Broccoli & Stilton Soup

I usually only have Stilton at Christmas, on gluten-free crackers. The only exception is when making this soup. It is really hearty and filling, and if you have the time to make herby, garlic croutons, they go really well with the Stilton.

 4 portions   **15 minutes**
Prepping the vegetables   **45 minutes**   **Yes**

Ingredients

- Large glug of sunflower oil
- 2 large onions, chopped
- 4 cloves of garlic, crushed
- Salt and pepper
- 640g broccoli including stems
- 1 x vegetarian, gluten-free stock cube (**celery**)
- 1 litre boiling water
- 4 bay leaves
- 220g Stilton cheese (**milk**)

Equipment

Chopping knife   Large saucepan   Garlic crusher

Measuring jug   Mixing spoon   Food blender

Method

1. Put the sunflower oil in a large pan, with the chopped onions and garlic, salt and pepper. Sweat everything off until the onions are looking golden.

2. Chop the broccoli florets and stems into smallish chunks and chuck them in the pan with the onions and stir for a minute or two.

3. Add a stock cube to the boiling water and pour it into the pan; the water should tickle the top of the broccoli. Season again by adding lots more salt and pepper. Add a few bay leaves to the pan (you'll need to take them out later, before blending so it helps to keep them tucked to the side of the pan so you can easily find them.) Put the lid on and cook until the broccoli is more than soft - for at least 20 minutes on a low heat so all the flavours can be absorbed into the water.

4. Once the soup is cooked and smelling good, blend it either using a food processor or hand-held blender. The more you blend it, the smoother it will taste. Add extra salt and pepper to taste and possibly a little water if the soup is really thick and you want to get more out of it.

5. Top the soup with some little chunks of freshly cut Stilton.

6. Store in an airtight tub in the fridge for 3 days.

Top Tips

Let the onions become caramelised before adding the broccoli. The right amount of seasoning is also key, so adjust accordingly before serving.

Allergens in bold

Roasted Butternut Squash, Red Pepper, Coconut & Chilli Soup

This soup takes a little longer than most, as you have to prepare and roast the butternut squash in the oven first. But it's worth it – and this recipe will produce a beautifully thick and filling soup. One of my absolute favourites in the colder months, really filling and satisfying, full of flavour and warmth.

 4 large portions   **1.5 hours**   **Yes**

Ingredients

- 1.17kg (1170g) peeled and chopped butternut squash
- 100ml sunflower oil + 2 tablespoons
- 1 x teaspoon dried mixed herbs
- 2 medium sized onions chopped
- 4 cloves of garlic, crushed
- Salt and lots of pepper
- 350g roasted red peppers drained from a jar or tin
- ¼ x teaspoon dried chili flakes
- 1 can of coconut milk/cream (400ml)
- 1 vegetarian, gluten-free stock cube (**celery**)
- 750ml boiling water
- Small handful of bay leaves

Equipment

Chopping knife   Large saucepan   Garlic crusher

Measuring jug   Mixing spoon   Food blender

Method

1. Pre-heat the oven to 190°C/350°F/gas mark 5 and line a large baking tray with parchment paper.

2. Peel the butternut squash and chop it into small cubes or wedges, discarding the seeds. Place the chunks of butternut squash in a large bowl with 2 tablespoons of sunflower oil, plenty of seasoning and 1 teaspoon mixed herbs. Toss the butternut squash pieces around in the bowl, to get them evenly covered in oil, herbs and seasoning, then tip them out onto the baking tray and roast them until they're soft with some added colour. The cooking time will vary depending on how big or small the pieces have been cut but will take at least 30 minutes in the oven.

3. Meanwhile, put 100ml sunflower oil in a large pan, with the chopped onions and garlic, salt and pepper and cook on medium heat until the onions are looking nice and golden. They're better to be slightly over cooked than under, in my opinion. Allow at least 15 minutes, stirring regularly.

4. Drain and then weigh and chop the red peppers and add them to the pan of cooked onions and cook for a further 10 minutes. Then add a ¼ teaspoon of chili flakes if you want a add a bit of a kick to the finished taste.

5. Once the butternut squash is cooked, add it to the pan along with 750ml of boiling water and a stock cube. Season again adding 1 x teaspoon of salt and plenty of cracked black pepper as well as a few bay leaves, tucked to the side of the pan (which you'll need to take out later). Put the lid on, leaving a small gap and cook on a low heat for another 10 minutes.

6. 6 Shake the tin of coconut milk and add the lot to the pan and leave to cook on a low heat for another 10 minutes. Then, take out the bay leaves and blend the soup to be as chunky or as smooth as you prefer, using a food processor or a hand-held blender. If you find the soup is a tad too thick just add a little more hot water and blend again. You may want to add a tad more salt and pepper to taste.

7. Store in the fridge in an airtight container for up to 3 days.

Carrot & Coriander Soup

I could never make soups. In fact, I had never tried to make soups. Big difference. After a good few years of making them both at home and the coffee shop, I can say I am a confident maker of soups! Hopefully you will be too, and once you know how to make a few flavours of soups, you'll probably not need to use a recipe book again! This soup is really thick and filling and you can dilute down a bit by adding more water and seasoning.

 6-8 portions   **15 minutes**   **45 minutes**   **Yes**

Ingredients

- Large glug of sunflower oil
- 3 medium onions chopped
- 3 cloves of garlic, crushed
- 1.5 kg carrots, peeled and chopped
- 1 vegetarian, gluten-free stock cube (**celery**)
- 60g / 1 small bunch fresh coriander
- 4 bay leaves
- Boiling water
- Salt and pepper

Equipment

Chopping knife   Large saucepan   Garlic crusher

Measuring jug   Mixing spoon   Food blender

Method

1. Heat the sunflower oil in the largest saucepan you have, and add the chopped onions and garlic, and a generous amount of salt and pepper. Sweat the onions until they are golden.

2. Peel and chop the carrots into chunks and chuck them in the pan with the onions and stir them around the pan so they can pick up flavour for about 5 minutes.

3. Add a stock cube to the pan and pour in enough boiling water so that it tickles the top of where the vegetables are. You want it to just about cover everything, but only just. Season again adding lots more salt and pepper. Add the chopped coriander, by roughly tearing it with your hands and include the stems.

4. Add a few bay leaves to the side of the pan (you'll need to take them out later, before blending so it helps to keep them tucked to the side so you can easily find them.) Put the lid on, allowing a little room for the steam to escape and cook until the carrots are nice and soft - for at least 20 minutes on a low heat.

5. Once the soup is smelling good, blend it – either using a food processor or hand-held blender. The more you blend it, the smoother it will taste. Add salt and pepper to taste and possibly a little water if the soup is really thick and you want to get more out of it.

6. Store airtight in the fridge for 3 days.

Pea & Mint Soup

A great soup for summer. My husband never thought he liked pea and mint soup until he tried this one. It's thick, so you can easily get more portions out of it if you wanted a lighter soup, by simply increasing the water content and adjusting the seasoning.

 4 large portions - 6 smaller portions **45 Minutes** **45 minutes** **Yes**

Ingredients

- Large glug of sunflower oil
- 200g white onions, chopped
- 2 cloves of garlic, crushed
- 700g frozen peas (weigh them frozen)
- 1 x litre boiling water
- 1 vegetarian, gluten-free stock cube (**celery**)
- 3 large bay leaves
- 15-20g fresh mint
- Salt and lots of cracked black pepper

Equipment

Chopping knife   Large saucepan   Garlic crusher

Measuring jug   Mixing spoon   Food blender

Method

1. Put the sunflower oil in a large pan, with the chopped onions and crushed garlic, on a low heat. Add salt and pepper and cook the onions until they're soft and golden.

2. Add the frozen peas to the pan of golden onions and regularly stir them around the pan so they can pick up the flavour, for about 5 to 10 minutes on a medium heat.

3. Then add the stock cube to the pan and pour in the boiling water. Season again adding lots more salt and pepper as well as adding a few bay leaves, to the side of the pan. Put the lid on, leaving a small gap and cook on a low heat for 10 minutes or so.

4. Add the fresh mint (but keep a tiny bit back as garnish, if you want), stems included. Just roughly tear it all up and using a large spoon "bob it" around in the pan of water and pop the lid back on, again, leaving a small gap. Leave it to cook on a low heat for another 10 minutes so that the mint can mingle into the peas and water.

5. Once the flavours are filling the room, blend it either using a food processor or hand-held blender. I think this soup tastes a lot better when it's really smooth and recommend it's blended for a while to make it as silky as possible and therefore a more refreshing and luxurious tasting soup. Add salt and pepper to taste and possibly a little water if the soup is really thick and you want to get more out of it, in which case once you've added extra water, blend it again. Serve with a little garnish of fresh mint.

6. Store in an airtight container, in the fridge for up to 3 days.

Allergens in bold

"Happy cakes" by Naomi Lowe

Sweet
Things

Bakewell Tarts

Ah, the trusty little Bakewell Tart! Crumbly pastry, the filling sweet and spongy with the combination of jam and frangipane filling. These taste like Bakewells should. I've had much feedback over the years from people saying how these are the best ever! I was never a fan of shop-bought Bakewells and gluten-free ones are hard to find anyway. So when my husband insisted on having home-baked ones I wasn't convinced, but they are one of my favourite things. Each one is like a little ray of sunshine.

18 tarts	**45 minutes** (including making the pastry)	**15–20 minutes at 165°C**	**30 minutes for resting & icing**	**Yes**

Ingredients

Pastry

- 235g Doves Farm gluten-free plain flour
- 125g vegan butter alternative
- 1 x teaspoon salt
- 1 medium **egg**
- 1 x tablespoon ice cold water

Frangipane Filling

- 100g soft dairy-free spread or vegan butter
- 100g icing sugar
- 100g ground **almonds** (**nuts**)
- 15g gluten-free plain flour
- 2 medium **eggs**
- ½ to ¾ jar of cherry or raspberry jam

Icing

- 220g icing sugar
- 35g water
- Glacé cherries to decorate

Equipment

(For pastry equipment see page 101)

Scales   Spatula   Measuring spoons

Medium bowl   Small bowl   Electric whisk

Piping bag   2 x 12 cupcake tins

Method

1. Make and roll out pastry as per pastry recipe on page 101 and blind bake the 18 little cases until they are golden.

2. Preheat the oven to 165°C/325°F/gas mark 3. For the frangipane mix, put the soft butter (or vegan alternative) and icing sugar in a bowl and mix together using a hand-held whisk or cake mixer, until light and fluffy. Add the ground almonds, followed by the plain gluten-free flour.

3. Finally add the eggs. It's really important that the eggs are not overworked as we don't want too much air getting in the mixture, so just mix them in enough so that they are incorporated evenly while not over beating them.

4. Put the jam in a bowl or piping bag and put a little dollop in the bottom of each pastry case: About a quarter of your case should be filled, leaving plenty of room for the frangipane mixture.

5. To add the frangipane mixture on top of the jam, either use a spoon or pop it into a piping bag and pipe it on. Fill the cases to the top of the edge of the pastry line.

6. Bake the Bakewells for 15–20 minutes. The cooking time will vary depending on how full your cases are. You'll know once they are cooked, as the filling will look a little golden and feel springy to the touch, rather than wet/wobbly. Once cooked, take them out of the oven and leave them to cool in their tins. Once they are completely cooled, gently take them out and prep the icing.

7. Fill a small bowl with icing sugar and a tiny bit of water. Mix until it's a really thick paste that has a small amount of slow movement when picked up with a spoon. If it's too stiff add a little water or if it's too runny add more icing sugar until you have the consistency you're happy with.

8. Easiest way to ice them is to put the icing sugar mix in a piping bag and pipe it on. Otherwise, use a teaspoon. Finally add the cherry on top and pop them in the fridge for the icing to harden up.

9. Store airtight either at room temperature or in the fridge for up to 7 days or in the freezer.

Allergens in bold

Bread Pudding
Mixed spices, cranberries and raisins

This is so easy to make and the idea is that you use any "unwanted" bread to make it. It's great if you have gluten-free bread that's about to go out of date but you can of course use fresh, purposefully bought bread for this. This "old fashioned style" bread pudding is full of flavor and warmth and is especially nice in the winter. A special thanks to Illaria, for this one - our first baker to join the team. You can also give this a twist by swapping the spices, raisins and cranberries for chocolate chip and apricot.

 8-10 Portions / 1x tray: (18cm wide x 27cm long and 2cm high)   **20 mins**   **30-40 minutes at 180°C**   **Yes**

Ingredients

- 310g gluten-free bread & crusts (usually contains **egg**)
- Zest of half an 1 orange
- 110g brown sugar
- 2.5 x tablespoon sweet mixed spice
- 135g raisins
- 90g dried cranberries
- 65g melted butter (**milk**)
- 310ml full fat **milk**
- 110ml cream (**milk**)
- 2 small **eggs**

Equipment

Scales

Parchment paper

Measuring spoons

Zester/ Grater

Large bowl

Small microwave safe bowl

Baking Tin*

Clingfilm

*18cm wide x 27cm long and 2cm high or more (about 7" wide, 11" long and 1" high)

Method

1. Generously line your tray with parchment paper, so it's coming up over the edges slightly. For this recipe I recommend using a popular tin size of 18cm wide x 27cm long and 2cm high or more. Alternatively you can use a smaller or bigger tin and adjust the cooking time.

2. Tear up the bread into little chunks and put them into a large bowl. Zest over half an orange. Add in the brown sugar, mixed spice and dried fruit.

3. Melt the butter in the microwave or on the hob and pour it over the bread, along with the milk, cream and eggs.

4. With clean hands or using plastic gloves, mush everything all together by hand, squeezing the mixture through your fingers until it's really well combined.

5. Tip the 'batter' in the lined tin, level out and cover with clingfilm and place in the fridge overnight. This helps intensify the flavour before cooking it the next day. Of course you can cook it straight away, but it's better if you can wait!

6. Preheat oven to 180°C/350°F/gas mark 4 and bake for between 30 minutes to 40 minutes until cooked. To check if it's cooked, use a skewer or sharp knife and check it comes out clean. You may want it a little more on the 'overdone side' to get the harder textures around the edges. If so, that's fine as this recipe is quite forgiving meaning the cooking times vary depending on your preference.

7. Once the bread pudding is out of the oven and cooled down, cut it into chunky portions. Enjoy straight away, on its own, or with ice cream. If you want to re-heat the bread pudding, it's better in the microwave rather than the oven.

8. Store any leftovers airtight in the fridge for up to 5 days or freeze.

Top Tip

To make a chocolate and apricot flavored one, replace the mixed spice, raisins and cranberries with:

- 135g cocoa nibs
- 90g dried, diced, apricot pieces.

Allergens in bold

Chocolate
Brownies

Brownies

This is one of the recipes that I used to make a lot soon after switching to a gluten-free diet and is thanks to my dear mum. These are really easy and quick to make, satisfyingly rich without being too sweet. Great paired with fruit and ice-cream. To make it dairy-free just swap the butter and chocolate for an alternative 'free-from' version.

 6 - 8 Portions
1 x 20cm x 20cm (8"x8") square tin   **15 minutes**   **20-24 mins at 180°C**   **Yes**

Ingredients

- 125g unsalted butter (**milk**)
- 125g dark chocolate, recommended 54% (check for **soya** and or **milk**)
- ½ x teaspoon salt
- ½ x teaspoon vanilla
- 150g caster sugar
- 80g cocoa powder
- 3 medium **eggs**
- ~~150g caster sugar~~
- ~~3 medium eggs~~

Equipment

 Scales   8" Square tin   Parchment paper

 Small saucepan   Medium glass bowl   Whisk

 Measuring spoons

Method

1. This recipe is based on using a square tin of around 20cm x 20cm. If you go for a much bigger or smaller tin, adjust the cooking time accordingly (cook for a little longer if the tin is smaller, or less time for bigger tins where the mixture would be more spread out).

2. Pre-heat the oven to 180°C/350°F/gas mark 4. Prepare the baking tin by brushing it with a little bit of oil or butter, and neatly cover it with parchment paper on the base and up the sides.

3. Weigh the butter and chocolate into a medium sized glass or metal bowl over a saucepan of hot water, on a low heat, making sure the hot water doesn't touch the bowl. Add salt and vanilla and stir regularly until everything has fully melted and becomes 'glossy'.

4. Take it off the heat and add the sugar, cocoa powder and eggs and give it a gentle but thorough mix. It's best that as little air as possible gets into the mixture when mixing it or you will have unwanted air pockets when baking. These brownies are best as flat, dense slabs! Once the mixture starts to become glossy again, almost gelatinous, it's ready to be poured into the tin. Level it out with a palette knife or your tool of choice.

5. Bake for between 20 to 24 minutes. If you like them on the fudgy side of cooked, take them out a little earlier. Once cool, carefully lift the brownie slab from the tin and cut to your preferred size.

6. Enjoy them at room temperature. Store airtight and in the fridge for up to 4 days or freeze.

Allergens in bold

Carrot Cake

This is honestly the best gluten-free carrot cake I have ever tasted. It's fresh, full of great ingredient combinations that all come together to create an exceptionally satisfying cake – no compromises here!

A nod to Ilaria, the first baker to work at the coffee shop; she played around with some recipes and hit the nail on the head with this one. And the smells this cake gives off when cooking is something else! Over the years, when the bakers and I would make this cake at the coffee shop, you could smell the sweet aroma of the cinnamon, carrots and coconut gently spilling out from the kitchen and on to the side street, alongside the sound of the coffee beans being ground, the humming of the ovens and customers commenting on the nice, welcoming smells. And here's how to make it.

10 or 12 portions 2 x 20cm (8")cake tins	**45 mins** including making the icing	**30 mins at 180°C**	**Yes**

Ingredients

- 125ml **milk** + half a juiced lemon
- 250ml sunflower oil
- 3 medium **eggs**
- 200g caster sugar
- 110g brown sugar
- 1 x tablespoon cinnamon
- 1 x tablespoon vanilla
- 1 x pinch salt
- 330g gluten-free self-raising flour
- 60g desiccated coconut flakes (**sulphites**)
- 330g finely grated carrots
- Optional - pumpkin and sunflower seeds to decorate the top.

Icing

- 60g butter (**milk**)
- 180g cream cheese (**milk**)
- Zest from large orange
- 500g icing sugar

Method

1. Line the two cake tins and pre-heat the oven to 180°C/350°F/gas mark 4.

2. Pour the milk into a jug and add the juice from half a lemon and let it sit for 10 minutes. The mixture will look like it's curdled – that's what we want!

3. In a large bowl, add oil, eggs, sugars, cinnamon, vanilla and salt. Whisk together either by hand or with a cake mixer, until everything is incorporated.

4. Add the gluten-free self-raising flour, coconut flakes and the finely grated carrots and mix them in. Finally pour in the milk and lemon mixture and thoroughly mix everything together to create a runny batter.

5. Evenly divide the batter across the two tins and bake them for 30 minutes. To ensure your sponge is moist (sorry for those of you who aren't fans of that word!!) it's really important this cake isn't overcooked, so it's a good idea to check it towards the end of the cooking time, with a skewer or sharp knife so you can take it out as soon as it's done.

6. Once cooked let the sponges cool down before removing them from their tins.

7. To ice, using a cake mixer or electric hand-held whisk, beat together the butter, cream cheese and orange zest. Slowly add in the icing sugar and beat until smooth and light. Once the sponges have completely cooled down they can be iced. The icing can be quite sticky against the sponges so it helps to dampen the palette knife or utensil you choose to use to spread on, as the little bit of water makes icing much easier. Finish the cake off with a sprinkling of sunflower and pumpkin seeds around the edge.

8. Keep it airtight in the fridge for up to 3 days or freeze.

Equipment

Scales	Parchment paper	Electric whisk

Large bowl	Measuring spoons	2x 8" cake tins

Zester/ grater

Chocolate & Orange Mousse Cake

I love chocolate and orange together and this is a great recipe. The sponge is light and the mousse is rich. I tested and tinkered with this recipe at home a few times before introducing it occasionally at the coffee shop. It's quick and easy to make but the mousse needs at least 3 hours in the fridge to set before you can dive into it!

 8 Portions
1 x 20cm (8") round cake

 30 minutes
plus 3 hours to set

 15 minutes at 180ºC

❄ **No**

Ingredients

Sponge

- 100g dairy-free spread
- 100g caster sugar
- 2 medium **eggs**
- 100g plain gluten-free flour
- 2 x tablespoon cocoa powder
- 1 x teaspoon baking powder

Mousse

- 200g dark, dairy-free chocolate (may contain **soya**)
- Grated rind/zest of 2 x oranges and juice from 1 of them
- 4 **egg** whites

Equipment

Scales

Parchment paper

Hand whisk

Medium bowl

Large bowl

Measuring spoons

8" cake tin

Zester/ grater

Spatula

Small saucepan

Method

1. Make sponge. Preheat oven to 180ºC/350ºF/gas mark 4 and line the base of a 20cm (8") cake tin with parchment paper.

2. Using the hand-held whisk, mix the dairy-free spread and sugar in a medium sized bowl until smooth and light. Add the eggs and mix again.

3. Add the flour, cocoa powder and baking powder and mix them together, making sure everything is well incorporated.

4. Pour the mixture into the cake tin and scrape the bowl down to avoid any wastage. Smooth the batter over with the back of a spoon so that the distribution is even throughout.

5. Bake for 15 minutes or a bit longer if not quite ready (check it using a skewer and make sure it comes out clean). Once baked, leave the cake sponge in the tin, not just to cool, but thereafter too, as you will need to add the mousse on top (once the cake is cooled) and you'll use the sides of the tin help to keep the mousse together while it sets.

6. Make mousse. You can do this while the sponge is cooking. Gently melt the chocolate in a glass bowl over a pan of hot water on a medium to low heat, making sure water doesn't touch the bowl. Add in the zest of 2 oranges and the juice from one of them and stir until melted. Then let this cool for 15 minutes.

7. In a separate bowl whisk the egg whites until they form stiff peaks. This will mean whisking vigorously for a few minutes and it's much easier using a cake mixer or electric hand-held whisk. If in doubt as to whether they are ready or not, you can try the old trick of putting the bowl upside down and checking to see that the egg whites stay in place without falling out of the bowl. Once ready, take a large spoonful and fold the egg whites into the chocolate mixture and gently fold in the remainder, carefully mixing it all together, being mindful not to over-do it or the mousse will lose volume.

8. Spoon the mousse mixture over the cooled sponge (that's still in its tin) and put the cake in the fridge for at least 3 hours to set. Once set, carefully remove it from the tin and enjoy!

9. Store the mousse cake in the fridge, airtight for up to 3 days.

Allergens in bold

Chocolate Cupcakes

No recipe book would be complete without cupcakes! This is the exact same recipe as for the vegan chocolate cake, only here there's the information you need to make the icing. The only allergen is soya. I've tried making these with almond and gluten-free oat milk, to see if the recipe can be soya-free. It does work, but if you have no objections to soya milk, I'd strongly recommend using it, as it produces a better texture and taste.

 12- 18 cupcakes (depending on how big you want them)   **20 mins**   **18 mins at 180°C**   **Yes**

Ingredients

Dry

- 140g gluten-free self-raising flour
- 150g caster sugar
- 35g cocoa powder
- 1.5 x tablespoon gluten-free ground flaxseeds
- ½ x teaspoon baking powder
- ½ x teaspoon salt

Wet

- 175ml **soya** milk
- 1.5 x teaspoon apple cider vinegar
- 60g olive oil

Chocolate Icing

- 50g dairy-free spread
- 50g dairy-free "butter" block (FLORA blocks are very good)
- 25g cocoa powder
- 350g sieved icing sugar
- And then add an additional flavour of your choice, from below (optional)

Icing flavour ideas that can work well on top of the above

- **Mocha** – add a bit of instant coffee with a splash of warm water and a dash of cocoa powder
- **Caramel** - 1 x tablespoon caramel syrup (used for coffees) plus 1 to 2 tablespoons water
- **Orange** – Zest of one orange
- **Peppermint** – 1 x teaspoon peppermint extract

Top tips:

For good tips on icing techniques YouTube and Instagram can be a great help. It's one of those things that comes with practice.

Method

1. To make the cupcake sponges, start by putting all the wet ingredients together in a jug and let them sit for 10 minutes to 'develop'. Pre-heat the oven to 180°C/350°F/gas mark 4.

2. Place cupcake cases in 12-hole cake tin.

3. In a medium bowl, put all the dry ingredients together and mix so that everything is nicely incorporated. Gently pour the wet mixture into the dry ingredients and thoroughly whisk until the batter looks nice and smooth. Let it sit in the bowl for 5 minutes. This allows it to thicken a little bit more.

4. Using an ice-cream scoop (the mechanical type, if you have one) scoop the batter evenly across the paper cases and bake for approximately 18 minutes. Bear in mind the cooking time depends on how big your cupcakes are, so keep a close eye towards the end of the cooking time. Use a skewer or knife to check it comes out clean.

5. Once cooked, leave them to cool completely before icing them.

6. Make the icing. I have found that using a mixture of two types of spread makes for a much nicer vegan icing: 50g of dairy-free soft spread (any type) plus 50g of a dairy-free and vegan style butter block, which must be soft. If you just have 1 type of spread or butter, rather than 2, then just use 100g of what you've got!

7. Put the soft "butter(s)" in a large bowl or cake mixer along with 350g icing sugar (sieve it first, if it's a bit lumpy). Then add the coca powder. To avoid a mini explosion of sugar and cocoa, it's a good idea to use a splash lid or tea-towel over the mixing bowl. Mix everything together continuously with the electric whisk until eventually all the ingredients come together to create an icing. You may need to add a small dash of water if the icing feels too dense. Or, if you have a caramel syrup for coffees, a glug of this in the icing makes it taste amazing!

8. You can add some additional flavour to the icing and mix it in, or use it as it is. If you have a piping bag and nozzle, pop the icing into the bag and ice your cupcakes or simply spread the icing on top using a spoon or small palette knife. They'll taste the same anyway! Fresh fruit and nuts are always nice on these too.

9. The cupcakes taste best the day they are made and kept at room temperature. If you don't use all the icing at once, store it in the fridge for up to 2 weeks. It will become very hard so next time you need to use it, it will need to loosening up using a mixer and by adding a dash more water or caramel syrup.

Equipment

 Scales   Measuring spoons   Electric whisk   Large bowl   Muffin cases

 Muffin tray   Ice-cream scoop   Sieve

Allergens in bold

Classic Chocolate Ganache Cake

This is one of the first cakes I enjoyed after realising I could no longer eat gluten. My mum used to make this for me by adapting our old family favourite chocolate cake, which she'd usually make for birthdays. Over time this recipe evolved to create a sponge that is rich in flavour by the addition of a little soya milk and banana; and although there is only a light hint of banana, it helps retain moisture in the cake. You can play around with this one, by swapping the chocolate ganache filling for a classic vanilla buttercream, and by using your favourite jam in the middle, and/or fresh fruit too.

 10/12 portions
2 x 20cm (8") cake tins

 30 minutes

 25 minutes at 170ºC

 Yes

Ingredients

- 250g butter (**milk**)
- 250g caster sugar
- 5 medium **eggs**
- 200g gluten-free self-raising flour (I recommend Doves Farm)
- 1 x teaspoon baking powder
- 75g cocoa powder
- 1.5 x tablespoons vanilla essence
- 1 x banana – blended to a pulp
- 50ml **soya** milk

Ganache Filling & Topping

- 200g dark chocolate (poss **soya**, **milk**)
- 150ml full fat crème fraiche (**milk**)

Jam Filling

- Generous lashings of raspberry jam for the centre, or you can try blackcurrant or cherry jam

Equipment

 Scales

 Parchment paper

 Cake mixer

 Large bowl

 Measuring spoons

 2x 8" cake tins

 Food blender

 Glass bowl

 Small saucepan

Method

1. Make the sponges. Heat the oven to 170ºC / 325ºF / gas mark 3. Lightly grease and line the base of the 2 tins. If you use different sized tins you may need to adjust the cooking time slightly.

2. Using a cake mixer, or hand-held electric mixer, beat the butter and sugar until light and fluffy. Mix in the eggs, followed by the flour, baking powder, cocoa powder and vanilla essence, and thoroughly mix until you have a smooth batter.

3. Blend the banana to a pulp using a food processor or hand-held blender until it's smooth. Then add the pulped banana and soya milk to the batter and mix it until it's silky and smooth once again.

4. Pour the mixture equally across both tins and level out, using the back of a spoon. Bake for 25 minutes. Check the sponges are cooked using a skewer or little knife, to make sure it's coming out clean and cooked throughout. They may need a little longer in the oven but be careful not to over-do them as the cocoa powder could make the cake a little dry if over cooked.

5. Make ganache. Break the chocolate up into small chunks and place the chocolate and in a glass bowl over a saucepan of hot water, on a low heat, making sure the hot water doesn't touch the bowl. Stir regularly until fully melted then take the bowl off the heat. Let this cool for 10 minutes before gently whisking in the crème fraiche by hand until evenly distributed.

6. Assemble the cake. When the chocolate sponges have cooled down, remove the parchment paper and spread a generous layer of raspberry jam (or your jam of choice) on the first sponge, followed by about half the ganache on top of the jam. Pop the second sponge on top and spread the top of the cake with the rest of the ganache. You may want to add fresh fruit and chocolate shavings to give it a wow factor!

7. Store airtight in the fridge for up to 3 days or freeze. Enjoy at room temperature.

Notes

You can make this cake bigger by using 2 x 25cm (10") tins and cooking the sponges for slightly less time.

Allergens in bold

Coffee & Walnut Cake

There were many trials and errors with this one over the first few years before finding a formula that worked time and time again and making it one of the most popular sponge cakes at the coffee shop. Many customers would tell the team and I that it's the best gluten-free coffee and walnut cake they'd ever tasted! I once shared this recipe with listeners on one of the local radio stations after being asked to share a great gluten-free cake recipe. The texture is beautiful and immensely satisfying. Even if you don't think you liked coffee and walnut cake, you have to try this one, it might convert you! This recipe works great for little cupcakes too, which of course won't need so long in the oven.

 10 portions
2 x 20cm (8") cake tins

 30 mins including making the icing

 20 mins at 180°C

 No

Ingredients

- 10g instant coffee. (Make sure it's a coffee that dissolves really well or it will affect the texture of your cake. Kenco Smooth Instant ground coffee is great.)
- 90ml hot water, in a little cup
- 200g soft butter (**milk**)
- 35g soft brown sugar
- 160g caster sugar
- 5 small **eggs**
- 140g gluten free self-raising flour (Doves Farm self-raising flour is great)
- ½ x tablespoon baking powder
- 1 x teaspoon xanthan gum
- 100g ground walnuts (**nuts**)

Icing

- 45g butter (**milk**)
- 135g cream cheese (**milk**)
- 400g icing sugar
- 3 x teaspoon instant coffee and a tiny splash of **milk** Mix until smooth.

Equipment

Scales   Parchment paper   Cake mixer

Large bowl   Measuring spoons   2x 8" cake tins

Food blender   Hand whisk   Palette knife

Method

1. Lightly grease and line the 2 tins and pre-heat oven to 180°C/350°F/gas mark 4.

2. Put 10g of instant coffee and 90ml hot water into a small cup. Thoroughly stir using a small spoon and leave to one side.

3. Using a cake mixer with the paddle beater beat the butter and sugars until light and fluffy. Crack in the eggs and mix them in.

4. In separate bowl, weigh the flour, baking powder and xanthan gum and add these to the batter. Ground the walnuts in food processor until they are well blended, being careful not to over-blend them or they will become too oily and then add these to the batter too. Mix until smooth and then add the wet coffee mixture from the cup. Continue beating slowly until you can see the mixture starting to look "elasticated".

5. Divide the batter equally between the two tins. Bake for 20-25 minutes and check the batter is cooked using a skewer. If it doesn't come out clean, give the sponges a few more minutes and then check them again. Once ready, let them sit in their tins and cool down.

6. Make icing. Mix the butter and cream cheese together with an electric hand-held mixer. Add in the icing sugar (sieve it first if it's lumpy) and keep mixing it in until it starts to resemble icing. In a little cup, measure 4 teaspoons instant coffee powder and a dash of milk and mix into a paste. Then add this to the icing and mix for a final time. Once the sponges are cool, they can be iced with a layer of icing in the middle and on top of the cake.

7. To make icing the cake a little easier to spread, pop a dollop of icing onto the sponge, then dip the palette knife in hot water and use it to spread the icing. Repeat until your cake is fully iced and decorate with pieces of walnuts around the sides. You can of course put the icing in a pretty cake nozzle and piping bag to create a neat finish.

8. Enjoy at room temperature but store airtight and in the fridge for up to 3 days.

Top tips:

You must use the right coffee powder such as Kenco instant coffee. When I've tried cheaper brands it has affected the texture of the sponge.

When mixing this cake, make sure the butter is soft and thoroughly mixed in. When doing the final mix once all the ingredients are in, focus on getting lots of air in there.

To work up the eggs, you need to keep beating the mixture until you can start to see the texture looking a little "elasticated". Usually you get this from cakes that contain gluten, but with gluten-free baking, you don't as there's no gluten. But with this recipe, thanks to a little xanthan gum and the eggs, we're able to mimic gluten and create a "stretchy" batter.

Allergens in bold

Crème Pâtissière Tarts

As soon as I learnt how to make pastry, these were the things I'd make time and time again before the coffee shop opened, when I was still dreaming of having a place that could sell delicious gluten-free bakes. As a little girl, when I lived in France (and before I could no longer eat gluten), I'd spend my pocket money on these, from local pâtisseries – the ones where you walk in and are graced with the sweet smell of hand-crafted pastries and freshly baked croissants. How I miss those!

Ingredients

Pastry

See pastry recipe (page 101)

Crème pâtissière

- 250ml of whole **milk**
- ½ half vanilla pod, or 1 teaspoon vanilla extract
- 50g of caster sugar
- 3 **egg** yolks
- 10g plain gluten-free flour
- 15g cornflour

Topping

Fruit of your choice

Glaze

- 100g caster sugar
- 100ml orange juice (or another flavour)

Equipment

(For pastry equipment see page 101)

Scales

Measuring jug

Saucepan

Large bowl

Measuring spoons

Tin sizes of your choice

Clingfilm

Sieve

Pastry brush

Whisk

Method

1. To make the pastry, see page 101 and think about what size you want your tarts to be. You can make a large one or lots of little ones. The case(s) that you want to fill with crème pâtissière must be blind-baked, golden, and completely cooled down.

2. Making the crème pâtissière requires full attention. For me, the pitfall is that it is sometimes not thick enough, and other times too runny or a bad texture. This recipe is intended to create a medium thick crème pâtissière, as pictured.

    Crème pat step 1 Put the milk and vanilla in the saucepan and bring to the boil. Use a thermometer if you have one. Take the milk off the heat as it comes to the boil and reaches 98C (208F). Keep an eye on the pan as the milk can boil over very quickly!

    Crème pat step 2 In a medium-sized glass bowl, whisk the sugar, egg yolks and flours together until thoroughly mixed and smooth.

    Crème pat step 3 Once the milk has boiled, pour a third of the warmed milk over the egg mixture and whisk vigorously until smooth and thoroughly combined.

    Crème pat step 4 Pour the egg mixture back into the saucepan with the rest of the milk and continue to whisk over a medium heat for 4 minutes.

    Crème pat step 5 Empty your crème pâtissière into a very fine meshed sieve, placed over a bowl or food storage box and using a whisk push the mixture through the sieve into the bowl/storage box. This helps to eliminate any last remaining lumps. Grab some cling film, place it directly on to the crème pâtissière to prevent a skin forming and leave it to cool for at least 4 hours in the fridge, allowing it to firm up a little more. It will last at least 3 days.

    Crème pat step 6 If you wanted a lighter pastry cream or want to make it go further, you can fold in whipped cream or crème Chantilly through the crème pâtissière. This is known as Crème Diplomat.

3. When you're ready to fill the pastry cases (having left the crème pâtissière to cool for 4 hours in the fridge) use a spoon or piping bag to fill the cases. Once the tarts are filled, top them with washed fruit of your choice.

4. You might want to glaze the fruit. It's really easy and gives them a shine. To make the glaze, which you can do in advance or while waiting for the crème pâtissière to cool down, put 100ml fruit juice and 100g caster sugar in a small pan on a low heat stirring regularly until the liquid starts to thicken. This can take upwards of 15 minutes. Once cool, the glaze can be used straight away or kept in the fridge for many weeks, in an airtight container.

5. To glaze the tarts, gently brush the fruits to give them a sheen, whilst being careful not to spoil the positioning of the fruits.

6. The stand-alone crème patissière will last 4 days, airtight and in the fridge. Once the tarts are filled they are best enjoyed within 2 days.

Top tips:

If you are lucky enough to have a Thermomix in your kitchen, then you can use the crème pâtissière recipe that pairs up with your machine. Doing it by hand does leave room for mistakes. I always feel a bit apprehensive making this by hand so hopefully, if you follow the recipe, you should be happy with the result.

Allergens in bold

Céline Lee - 2017

Dark Chocolate Cake

In 2016, towards the end of a long hot summer, Céline (pictured) came to the UK from Paris and joined the small team as a Baker and stayed until the end of 2017 when she left to pursue her very own, stunning food business: Cocolico Patisserie. She has a real passion for food, especially vegan baking; she'd say it's like a science. Not only did I learn a lot from working with her, but I also got to practise my French a little! She created this delicious sponge cake; gluten-free and vegan. It's a great recipe that you can easily replicate at home to make a beautiful 3-layer cake or lots of cupcakes.

---

 10 portions
3 x 20cm (8") for a cake with 3 layers

 20 mins

 18 mins at 180°C

 Yes

Ingredients

Wet

- 350ml **soya** milk
- 1.5 x tablespoon apple cider vinegar
- 120g olive oil

Dry

- 285g gluten-free self-raising flour
- 300g caster sugar
- 75g cocoa powder
- 3 x tablespoon ground flaxseeds
- ½ x tablespoon baking powder
- 1 x teaspoon salt

Ganache

- 170g dairy-free cocoa nibs, ideally 54%, (may contain soya depending on the brand you use)
- 60ml **soya** milk
- 30g coconut oil
- 1 x pinch of salt

Chocolate icing (optional extra)

- 25g dairy-free spread
- 25g dairy-free "butter" block (FLORA blocks are very good)
- 15g cocoa powder
- 175g sieved icing sugar
- Small dash of water

Method

1. If you have 3 cake tins, I recommend you split this across those tins, rather than just using 2. But if you do have just 2 tins, use the same quantities of ingredients as described here, but cook the sponges for a little longer, as they will be a bit thicker than if spread over 3 tins.

2. Line the bottom of your tins with a circle of parchment paper to the edge and pre-heat the oven to 180°C/350°F/gas mark 4.

3. In a big jug, put all the wet ingredients together and allow them to sit for 10 minutes. It's really important to let the wet ingredients sit so that they have time to react and thicken, which in turn means you'll end up with a better cake.

4. In a medium bowl, put all the dry ingredients together and mix so that everything is nicely incorporated. Gently pour the wet mixture into the dry ingredients and thoroughly whisk until the batter looks nice and smooth. Let it sit for 5 minutes.

5. Then pour it evenly across the 2 or 3 cake tins and bake for 18 minutes or possibly a bit longer if you're using 2 tins. Check the sponges are cooked using a skewer and making sure it comes out clean before taking them out. Leave the sponges to cool.

6. Make ganache. This takes just 5 minutes so only make it once your sponges are cooled and ready to be covered in chocolate! Put all the ganache ingredients in a small saucepan on a low heat and mix until smooth, stirring frequently.

7. Assemble the sponge. Take the cooled sponges out of their tins and remove the parchment paper. Place the first one on a plate and add a good dollop of raspberry jam (or a red/dark jam of your choice), then spoon on a third of the freshly made chocolate ganache and repeat with the second layer. For the top layer, omit the jam and just pour over the rest of the ganache. It's runny when it's just been made but it soon hardens up. You can add fruit on top and in the layers too or even a vegan buttercream.

8. Optional - Make the icing. Put the soft "butter(s)" in a large bowl or cake mixer along with the icing sugar. Then add the cocoa powder an a dash of water and mix everything together continuously with an electric whisk until eventually all the ingredients come together. Pop the icing in a piping bag with pretty nozzle and pipe the icing around the sides.

9. It's best enjoyed within 2 days and stored at room temperature. Suitable for the freezer too.

Equipment

| Scales | Measuring spoons | Electric whisk | Large bowl | Parchment paper | 3x 8" cake tins | Saucepan | Glass bowl |

Allergens in bold

Ilaria Marsigli - 2014

Date, Beetroot & Chocolate Cake

A cake like no other! This is a really "grown-up" cake. It's dairy-free and has no refined sugar and is intensely rich and gooey. First made by Ilaria (pictured), during the very early days of the coffee shop first opening it was an instant hit with our customers and is great with coffee or enjoyed at home with a glass of red wine. And if you don't plan on eating the whole lot in the space of a few days, then it's a good idea to freeze some. Best way is to freeze individual slices so that they defrost quicker and therefore you can enjoy it as and when you need a "pick-me-up".

10/12 portions 1x 25cm (10") cake	**40 mins**	**50 mins to 1 hr at 180°C**	**Yes**

Ingredients

- 530g pitted dates
- 330ml boiling water
- 250g cooked beetroot (not vinegared), drained
- 170ml olive oil
- 1 x teaspoon gluten-free tamari sauce (**soya**)(Tamari is gluten-free soy sauce)
- 1 x teaspoon vanilla essence
- 6 medium **eggs**
- 170g cocoa powder
- 1 x tablespoon baking powder
- 1 x handful pumpkin seeds to decorate
- 1 x handful sunflower seeds to decorate

Equipment

Scales

Parchment paper

Electric whisk

Large bowl

Measuring spoons

10" cake tin

Food blender

Spatula

Saucepan

Method

1. Pre-heat the oven to 180°C/350°F/gas mark 4. Weigh out the pitted dates and pop them in a saucepan on a medium heat, covered with 330ml boiling water. Stir regularly until the water has been completely absorbed by the dates and they've become soft. This will take about 20 minutes or so.

2. Meanwhile, drain and weigh the cooked beetroot and pop it in a food processor and blend until it's a smooth pulp. Once done, tip it into a large bowl.

3. Measure the olive oil, tamari, vanilla and eggs and add these to the bowl of beetroot and mix. You can do this either by hand or using a cake mixer. Now add the cocoa powder and the baking powder and give everything another mix.

4. Once the dates have absorbed all the water and are soft, pop them in the food processor and blend them to a pulp, just like you did with the beetroot, and then add them to the large bowl with all the other ingredients and thoroughly mix everything together.

5. Pour the mixture into the cake tin. Sprinkle the top of the cake with seeds of your choice, such as pumpkin and sunflower seeds and bake until the cake feels firm, for around 50 minutes, possibly a tad more, depending on the oven. You will find that the cake will stay very dense and wet in the middle for quite some time, so please don't panic if you check it and it still feels undercooked. It all comes together towards the end of the cooking time. Once you're happy with it, double check it's cooked in the middle using a skewer or small knife to make sure it comes out clean. Once ready, take it out of the oven and allow it to cool. The cake can be enjoyed warm or cold. To reheat, pop each slice in the microwave for bout 30 seconds.

6. Store airtight in the fridge for up to 4 days or freeze.

Top tip:

Put parchment paper on the base and a separate strip around the rim of the tin. Using parchment paper will help act as a barrier when cooking - the cocoa powder in the cake mixture is prone to overcooking on the edges and then becomes bitter. Because this cake is so dense, the cooking time is long, so it's important the cake is well cooked in the middle, whilst not tasting overdone on the sides. Using parchment paper is the best way to protect it.

Allergens in bold

Fluffy Scones

When I first opened the gluten-free coffee shop, I'd written off ever producing quality scones simply because I'd yet to taste a decent one. But with some trials and errors and thanks to the persistence and determination from our baker at time, Ilaria, we started producing beautiful, fluffy scones with many customers coming back especially for them, many of whom weren't coeliac or on a gluten-free diet. An elderly gentleman once said that these took him straight back to Cornwall and that he'd tried many scones in his time and that these were most certainly the best he'd ever tasted. The recipe's been kept under lock and key until now and I'm so happy to finally share it with you. Enjoy! And if you need to make the scones vegan, head to page 109.

 10 scones   **20 mins**   **16-22 minutes at 180°C**   **Yes**

Ingredients

Wet

- 2 medium **eggs**
- 150ml double cream (**milk**)
- 150ml **milk**
- 2 ½ x teaspoon freshly squeezed lemon juice

Dry

- 100g soft unsalted butter (**milk**)
- 500g gluten-free self raising flour
- 50g caster sugar
- 2 x teaspoon baking powder
- 1 x teaspoon xanthan gum
- 1 x teaspoon salt

Egg Wash

- 1 x **egg** yolk and splash of **milk** for egg wash

Equipment

Scales

Electric whisk

Measuring jug

Large bowl

Measuring spoons

Pastry brush

Sieve

Ice-cream scoop

Flat baking tray

Method

1. Pre-heat the oven to 180°C/350°F/gas mark 4 and line a large baking tray with parchment paper.

2. In a jug, combine all the wet ingredients and leave to one side to 'develop' for 10 minutes.

3. Meanwhile, using an electric hand-held whisk or cake mixer, add the soft butter from the dry ingredients to a large bowl and sieve over half of the flour. Sieving the flour makes the scones fluffier. Mix the flour and butter on a low setting until it's crumbly and starts to resemble slightly damp sand. Then add the rest of the sieved flour along with the sugar, baking powder, xanthan gum and salt, and mix it all together once again.

4. Gently add the wet ingredients to the dry using a mixer and thoroughly mix them together on a medium to high speed until you have a smooth looking batter. Using an ice-cream scoop or spoon, pop 2 dollops on top of one another, straight on to the lined baking tray, leaving at least 5cm gaps between the scones, so they have room to expand in the oven. Before baking them, if you'd like to add a dash of extra colour to them, make an egg wash by mixing together a splash of milk and 1 egg yolk into a little cup/bowl. Using a pastry brush, dip it in and lightly brush the top of the scones.

5. Bake for between 16-22 minutes, turning the tray around half way through the bake to ensure they are evenly cooked. The cooking time will vary from oven to oven, so keep an eye on them towards the end and check them using a skewer or sharp knife to make sure it comes out clean.

6. Allow to cool for about 10 minutes and enjoy. They are best enjoyed warm. To re-heat them, pop each scone in the microwave for 20 seconds or so.

7. Enjoy within 2 days. Store airtight and at room temperature or freeze.

Allergens in bold

Frangipane Tart

First, you need to know how to make amazing gluten-free pastry: see page 101. Once you've got your head around that, and have practiced, you can use the pastry recipe to make cases of all shapes and sizes, for sweet and savoury things including frangipane tarts, and experiment with different flavours. The list is endless and here are some winning combinations to choose from. What this recipe will do is give you the base recipe for making the frangipane filling; it's then up to you to add the flavours you want, using fruit, chocolate, nuts etc.

Ingredients

Pastry

- 235g Doves Farm gluten-free plain flour
- 125g **butter** (frozen into chunks)(**milk**) or dairy-free butter alternative
- 1 x teaspoon salt
- 1 medium **egg**
- 2 x tablespoon ice cold water (only 1 x tablespoon if making the pastry dairy-free)

Frangipane filling

- 130g soft **butter** (**milk**) or dairy-free alternative
- 130g icing sugar
- 130g ground **almonds** (nuts)
- 25g gluten-free plain flour
- 3 medium **eggs**

Equipment

(For pastry equipment see page 101)

Scales

10" flan tin

Measuring spoons

Electric whisk

Large bowl

Spatula

Method

1. Make and roll out the pastry as per pastry recipe and blind bake in your chosen tin size, until golden: see page 101.

2. Once the pastry is golden and ready to be filled, pre-heat the oven to 165°C/325°F/gas mark 3.

3. Put the soft butter (or vegan alternative) and icing sugar in a bowl and mix together using a hand-held whisk or cake mixer, until light and fluffy. Add the ground almonds, followed by the plain gluten-free flour.
Finally add the eggs. It's really important that the eggs are not overworked as we don't want too much air getting in the mixture, so just mix them in enough so that they are incorporated evenly whilst not over-beating them.

4. Flavour combinations – choose one. Once you've blind-baked your pastry and have the frangipane mixture ready, you now come to the most important decision - what flavours to add? This could be seasonal fruit, or what you have in your store cupboard. Here are some ideas for flavour combinations I love:

Blueberry and lemon
200g fresh or frozen blueberries – you can have as many or as few as you want, along with the zest of 1 lemon. Simply add these ingredients to the frangipane mixture and mix, then fill the pastry case.

Summer berries and orange
200g fresh or frozen mixed berries and zest of 1 orange or lemon. Just add these ingredients to the frangipane mixture and mix, then fill the pastry case.

Raspberry and peach
100g fresh or frozen raspberries, and 150g chopped peaches, either fresh or tinned. These just need to be added to the frangipane mixture before using it to fill the pastry case.

Cranberry and white chocolate
150g dried cranberries, 150g white chocolate pieces, added into the frangipane mixture.

Apricot and chocolate
Smother chocolate spread over the base of the tart. Sprinkle with up to 150g dried and diced apricot pieces. Fill the tart with the frangipane mixture, then add a generous sprinkling of chocolate nibs (either white, milk or dark) on top.

Plum and ginger (my favourite)
4 plums cut into little chunks. Place half of them onto the pastry. Add 2 tablespoons of stem ginger cut into tiny little pieces or grated, and evenly distribute throughout the frangipane mixture. Then top the tart with the rest of the plum pieces and sprinkle flaked almonds on top (optional).

Pear/apple and chocolate (or chocolate spread!)
3 pears (or apple) diced, 150g dark chocolate coca nibs or spread a thick layer of chocolate spread to the base of the pastry. Add small slices of pear or apple in the frangipane mixture, saving some to use for decorating the top of the tart.

5. Once you've decided on the flavour fill the tart making sure there isn't any spillage over the edge of the pastry and the baking tin. The mixture will rise a little in the oven. Bake for around 45 minutes, checking regularly after that. The cooking time will vary depending on the flavour combinations (some are wetter than others) and also how full your case is.

6. A good way to check if it's cooked is to see if it still has a bit of a 'wobble' to it. If it does, bake it for a bit longer to ensure that the eggs in the frangipane mixture are cooked. Once cooked and cool, take it out of the tin and enjoy!

7. Store airtight in the fridge for up to 4 days or freeze.

Allergens in bold

Granola Bars

Once cooked, these chunky and dense granola bars need to be left to set in the fridge for at least 6 hours before you can cut into them. But it's worth the wait. They are like a meal replacement when you're on the go; they can be frozen too, so you can make a batch and pop them in the freezer (pre-cut) and you have a quick snack to save you time. You can also add chocolate over these to give them an 'upgrade'.

 10/12 bars
1x tray: 18cm x 27cm long and 2cm high or more (7" wide, 11" long and 1" high)

 20 mins

 15-20 mins at 170°C

 Yes

Ingredients

Dry

- 80g roughly chopped **almonds** or **pecans (nuts)**
- 60g roughly chopped dried apricots (**sulphates**)
- 100g sultanas or raisins
- 50g pumpkin seeds
- 20g sunflower seeds
- 15g **sesame** seeds
- 50g ground **almonds (nuts)**
- 400g gluten-free oats
- 1.5 x teaspoon ground cinnamon

Wet

- 80g dairy-free spread
- 80g melted coconut oil
- 140g golden syrup
- 160g light brown soft sugar

Equipment

Scales	Measuring spoons	Baking tray
Large bowl	Rolling pin	Saucepan

Parchment paper

Method

1. Pre-heat the oven to 170°C/325°F/gas mark 3. Line your baking tray with parchment paper leaving enough to come up and over the sides of the tin – it will help to enable you to easily lift the granola slab from the tray once it's cooled down. If using a tin that's significantly different in size to the tin size used for this recipe, you may want to adapt the ingredients and/or the cooking time accordingly.

2. Weigh all the dry ingredients and put them in a large bowl and mix them by hand.

3. Put all the 'wet' ingredients in a small pan and melt them together on the hob, on a medium heat, making sure you don't let it boil, stirring regularly. Once everything is melted, take the liquid mixture off the heat and pour/scrape it into the bowl of dry ingredients. Using a spoon, mix the whole thing together until it's all thoroughly combined, making sure to reach the bottom of the bowl and that the mixture looks evenly wet and sticky throughout.

4. Now tip the mixture into the lined baking tray and press it down. If you've used the same tin as suggested here, it may seem like it won't all fit, but it does. Just keep pressing it all in. And if you can, lay a piece of parchment paper over the top to flatten and compact the mixture even more, using a small rolling pin.

5. Bake it in the pre-heated oven for 15 to 20 minutes - it's best not to overcook this one as it continues to cook a little once it's taken out of the oven. If you like your granola bars a little chewy, reduce the cooking time a tad. If you prefer them to be a bit tougher and with a little crunch on the side, cook them a little longer.

6. Once the granola slab is cooked, let it cool down a little before placing the tray in the fridge for at least 6 hours or overnight, to harden.

7. Once it's hardened up in the fridge, it's ready to be cut. If you're using the tin size recommended in this recipe, then cutting the slab into 10 or 12 individual portions gives a lovely size.

8. Once cut, keep them airtight and in the fridge. These last a good month. Can also be frozen.

Allergens in bold

Hazelnut, Chocolate & Coffee Sponge Cake

This is a heavenly combination of flavours. This recipe comes off the back of the coffee and walnut cake recipe. The walnuts and coffee have simply been swapped for hazelnuts and chocolate, but keeping the coffee icing really gives this an extra dimension of flavour. The sponge is very bouncy and is the closest thing to how I remember cakes tasting before having to say good-bye to gluten. This can be made dairy-free by swapping all the dairy products for dairy-free alternatives.

Ingredients

Chocolate Ganache Top

- 185g milk chocolate (**milk**)
- 22g butter (**milk**)
- 150g double cream (**milk**)

Coffee Icing

- 40g butter (**milk**)
- 120g cream cheese (**milk**)
- 360g icing sugar
- 2 x teaspoon instant coffee and a tiny splash of **milk**. Mix until smooth

Sponges

- 200g butter (**milk**)
- 30g brown sugar
- 170g caster sugar
- 5 medium **eggs**
- 100g ground **hazelnuts** (**nuts**)
- 135g gluten-free self-raising flour
- 1 x teaspoon baking powder
- 1 x teaspoon xanthan gum
- 1 x tablespoon hot chocolate powder or cocoa powder mixed in a small cup with 85ml warm milk (**milk**)

Equipment

Scales   Measuring spoons   Saucepan

Large bowl   2x 8" cake tins   Palette knife

Parchment paper   Electric whisk   Piping bag

Method

1. First make the chocolate ganache topping. This layer of rich chocolate will be spread on top of the sponge but needs at least 4 hours to set before it can be used. So make this in advance. It takes less than 15 minutes to do.

2. Weigh the chocolate and break it into small pieces and place it in a small glass bowl along with the butter. Place the bowl over a pan of water, on a medium heat, and make sure the water doesn't touch the bowl. Once the butter and chocolate have melted, add the double cream and gently stir it in until it's the same colour and consistency throughout. Now place the ganache in an airtight container and into the fridge for at least 4 hours to set, before it can be used on the top of the sponge.

3. Make the coffee icing. This will sit in the middle of the cake and you can make it in advance or once the cake is ready to be iced. Mix the butter and cream cheese together with an electric hand-held mixer. Mix in the icing sugar, and sieve it first, if it's lumpy. Finally add the instant coffee paste and mix a final time. If you want a slightly stiffer icing, just make a small increase to the amount of icing sugar.

4. Preheat the oven to 180°C/350°F/gas mark 4. Make sponges. Use a hand-held electric whisk or cake mixer and beat together the butter and sugars until light and fluffy. Mix in the eggs.

5. Blend the hazelnuts in a food processor until they are fine and crumb-like. Add these to the batter, along with the flour, baking powder and xanthan gum and mix together again.

6. Finally warm some milk in the microwave or in a small pan and add the hot chocolate/cocoa powder and mix together, then add this to the batter. Mix for one last time at medium speed until smooth with the mixture starting to look a little "elasticated".

7. Line the base of the two round baking tins with parchment paper and divide the batter equally between them.

8. Bake for 40 minutes and check the sponges are cooked by using a skewer or sharp knife to make sure it comes out clean. The sponges might need to be left in for a few more minutes. Once ready, let them cool and then remove them from their tins.

9. Ice the cake. Remove any baking paper from the sponges. Place one sponge on to a plate and spread the coffee icing over the sponge. To help make it easier to ice, you can use a wet palette knife by dipping it in hot water and using it to spread the icing.

10. Now place the other sponge on top of the coffee icing so that the coffee icing is now sandwiched between the two layers of cake.

11. Check that the chocolate ganache is set, and evenly spread this on to the top layer. You may want to now add any leftover coffee icing to the top of the cake, using a pretty piping nozzle and sprinkle any spare hazelnuts on top, too.

12. Best eaten at room temperature and store airtight in the fridge for up to 3 days.

Allergens in bold

Lemon Meringue Tart

This one is a bit special and can be dairy-free too, if using dairy-free spread rather than butter. It's all about the lemon curd sandwiched between the crumbly pastry and the sweet, soft meringue. Great as a large tart or mini and medium sized ones work well too, using whatever sized tins you have. They always look so delicate and old fashioned. The tart pictured was made for my husband in spring 2020, when I first started writing the recipe book.

Ingredients

Pastry

This will produce 1 x batch of pastry to fill a 25cm (10") flan dish or 18 miniature ones

- 235g Doves Farm gluten-free plain flour
- 125g vegan butter alternative
- 1 x teaspoon salt
- 1 medium **egg**
- 1 x tablespoon ice cold water

Lemon Curd

- 5 x tablespoon freshly juiced lemons, along with the zest from the lemon(s)
- 80g dairy-free spread or vegan butter
- 120g caster sugar
- 3 large **eggs** whisked

Italian meringue

- 200g caster sugar
- 50ml water
- 100g **egg** whites

Equipment

(For pastry equipment see page 101)

Scales

10" flan tin

Measuring spoons

Glass bowl

Large bowl

Spatula

Saucepan

Whisk

Zester/grater

Hand whisk

Piping bag

Sieve

Kitchen thermometer

Blow torch

Method

1. There are three stages to this recipe. All are quite quick in isolation. The one component that takes the longest is the lemon curd, due to the time it needs to rest which is at least 6 hours or overnight, in the fridge. Otherwise, the gluten-free pastry is quick once you're pretty confident at it. Once the pastry and lemon curd is made, the meringue is really quick.

2. Make pastry. Head over to page 101 to see how to make the pastry. You'll then need to roll the pastry out and use it to fill the 25cm metal dish or smaller tins if you prefer. Blind bake the pastry until golden in colour. This will create a crumblier pastry.

3. Make the lemon curd. Prepare the lemon juice by firstly zesting the lemons and then squeezing the juice from a couple of lemons, so you end up with enough juice for 5 tablespoons. Put the zest and the juice in a cup or bowl, and set to one side.

4. Melt the dairy-free butter in a glass bowl over a pan of water on medium to low heat, making sure the water doesn't touch the bowl. Once melted, add 5 tablespoons of the fresh lemon juice and zest.

5. Then add the sugar and stir using a whisk. When the sugar no longer feels "grainy", quickly whisk in the eggs.

6. Keep the hob on a low heat and whisk the curd regularly and it will start to thicken up. I recommend giving it a little mix every 3 minutes. The cooking time for the curd will take at least 30 minutes, or a little longer if you want a thicker curd.

7. Once you're happy with the thickness of the curd (and bear in mind it will be a bit thicker once it's set and had time to cool down in the fridge), take it off the heat. To create smooth lemon curd, it's well worth straining it through a fine mesh sieve, placed over a bowl. Once strained, you'll see little 'bits' caught in the mesh and what is left is really smooth curd. Cover the curd with the cling-film (or similar) by placing it directly on to the curd; this helps prevent a little skin from forming. Place it in the fridge to set for at least 6 hours or overnight.

8. Make the Italian meringue. Put the sugar and water into a small saucepan over a medium heat with a thermometer resting in the liquid.

9. Meanwhile, in a medium or large sized bowl whisk the egg whites with an electric whisk until you can see small peaks forming. To check they have been whisked enough, turn the bowl upside down and if the egg whites stay put, it's perfect.

10. Heat the water and sugar until it reaches between 118°C and 121°C (you'll need to rest a thermometer probe in the pan) then take it off the heat and slowly pour it into the bowl of egg whites whilst whisking.

11. Turn the whisk up to full speed and whisk until the mixture has cooled down to room temperature. This will take a few minutes. The meringue is now ready to use and requires no more cooking.

12. Assemble the cake. Once the pastry is blind baked and golden, the curd is set and ready to be used, and the Italian meringue is also ready, the cake can be assembled. Smother the lemon curd on the pastry case(s). Put the meringue on top, using a piping bag or by simply spreading it on. If you have a blow torch, use it to define the textures in the meringue and give it a hint of colour.

13. The tart(s) will last 2 to 3 days in the fridge but are best the day they are made as the pastry will be at its crumbliest.

Lemon Sponge
with Lemon Curd

A classic - lemon sponge and home-made lemon curd. This recipe is thanks to my incredible mum. She helped with the baking when we first opened and would make this along with some of the other sponge cakes. She would travel down to Reading on the train from London in the evenings, and work until the early hours of the morning so this cake was fresh for the next day. If you like lemon cake, you must give this a try.

10 portions
2 x 20cm (8") cake
tins for the two layers

 1 hour, including
making the curd

 25–30 mins at 170°C

❄ **Yes**

Ingredients

Lemon curd

- 80g dairy-free spread or vegan butter
- 5 x tablespoons freshly squeezed lemon juice & zest
- 120g caster sugar
- 3 medium **eggs**, whisked

Sponge

- 300g dairy-free spread or vegan butter
- 300g caster sugar
- 6 medium **eggs**
- 300g gluten-free self-raising flour
- 6 x tablespoons of freshly squeezed lemon juice and the zest

Equipment

Scales	Measuring spoons	Electric whisk

2x Medium bowl	Small pan	2x 8"cake tins

Grater	Parchment paper	Strainer

Clingfilm

Top Tips

If you have any leftover lemon juice, pour it over your finished sponges when they come out of the oven. To make the cake look fancy, add some meringue around the top.

Method

1. This cake requires a little planning as the lemon curd needs at least 6 hours to set in the fridge before it can be spread over the sponge. You can either make the curd first (it can easily last up to 10 days in the fridge, stored in an airtight container). Or you can make the lemon curd while the sponges are cooking in the oven and then assemble them at least 6 hours later or the next day.

2. Prepare the lemon juice by zesting and squeezing all the zest and juice from about 5 lemons: the number of lemons needed will depend on their size, but in total you will need 11 tablespoons worth (6 tablespoons for the sponges and 5 tablespoons for the lemon curd). Put the zest and juice in a cup or bowl, and set to one side; this will be used in both the sponge and the curd.

3. Make lemon curd. Melt the dairy-free butter in a glass bowl over a pan of water on medium to low heat, making sure the water doesn't touch the bowl. Once melted, add 5 tablespoons of the fresh lemon juice and zest.

4. Then add the sugar and stir using a whisk. When the sugar no longer feels "grainy", quickly whisk in the eggs.

5. Keep the hob on a low heat and whisk the curd regularly and it will start to thicken up. I recommend giving it a little mix every 3 minutes. The cooking time for the curd will take at least 30 minutes, or a little longer if you want a thicker curd.

6. Once you're happy with the thickness of the curd (and bear in mind it will be a bit thicker once it's set and had time to cool down in the fridge), take it off the heat. To create smooth lemon curd, it's well worth straining it through a fine mesh sieve, placed over a bowl. Once strained, you'll see little 'bits' caught in the mesh and what is left is really smooth curd. Cover the curd with the cling-film (or similar) by placing it directly on to the curd; this helps prevent a little skin from forming. Place it in the fridge to set for at least 6 hours or overnight.

7. Make sponges. Lightly grease and line the 2 x 20cm (8") tins and pre-heat oven to 170°C/325°F/gas mark 3.

8. Beat together the dairy-free spread and sugar into a large bowl or cake mixer until light and fluffy. Stir in the eggs, followed by flour and 5 tablespoons of the freshly squeezed lemon juice and zest. Thoroughly mix everything together until the batter looks smooth.

9. Pour the mixture evenly into both tins and level out with the back of a spoon. Bake the sponges for 25 minutes. Check the sponge is cooked by inserting a skewer or sharp knife into the centre to see if it comes out clean and free of batter. It might need a few more minutes.

10. Once cooked, remove from the oven. While still hot, if you have any spare lemon juice, drizzle a little around the sides and middle of the sponges.

11. Once the sponges have totally cooled down, and the lemon curd has had time to set, generously spread the middle layer with the lemon curd.

12. Best enjoyed within 2 days and stored airtight in the fridge. Any spare lemon curd will last up to 10 days in the fridge, if airtight.

Millionaire Shortbread

Of course, there are three stages to this recipe and it's important to get all of them right to achieve a great millionaire shortbread. So with this in mind, I have tried to write the recipe as clearly as possible so that you can make this at home and be really proud of the result. It's important to mention that the caramel, once made and spread over the base, has to be left to cool down completely, which takes a few hours, or it can be sped up by putting the tray in the freezer for an hour or so. In any case, it means from start to finish, this recipe requires time and patience. But I promise it is worth it. The buttery, crunchy, slightly salty base is divine even on its own. You can easily swap some of the ingredients for dairy-free alternatives although when it comes to the caramel, I am yet to successfully create a dairy-free version that has the same level of density both in taste and texture.

 10/12 portions
18cm wide x 27cm long
(7"x11" and 1" high)

 20 minutes - base
10-12 minutes - caramel
5 minutes - ganache

 20-25 mins at
180°C base only

 Yes

Ingredients

Shortbread

- 225g butter in small chunks (**milk**)
- 55g caster sugar
- 55g icing sugar
- ½ x teaspoon vanilla
- 50g corn flour
- 65g polenta
- 225g rice flour
- ½ x teaspoon salt

Caramel

- 397g x condensed **milk** (standard size tin)
- ½ x teaspoon salt
- 2 x tablespoon golden syrup
- 75g brown sugar
- 75g unsalted butter (**milk**)
- Chocolate topping
- 100ml double cream (**milk**)
- 100g dark chocolate 54% cocoa nibs or squares of chocolate, broken up (**milk**, possibly **soya** too)
- 4 x squares white chocolate (**milk**, **soya**)

Method

1. Make the biscuit base. Pre-heat the oven to 180°C/350°F/gas mark 4 and check the size of the tin you're using against the one recommended here. If the tin you're using differs a lot, adjust the ingredients proportionately across the 3 stages of the millionaire shortbread.

2. Line the tin with parchment paper. Be really generous – you want the paper to come up on all four corners by an additional 5cm (about 2").

3. Weigh all the shortbread ingredients into a bowl and make sure the butter is soft. Thoroughly mix them all together using a cake mixer or an electric hand-held whisk. Once the mixture is thoroughly combined, tip it into the tin and spread it to all four corners and create an even distribution. It's easiest to use your hands or the back of a spoon to smooth it out throughout. Bake for 20-25 minutes until golden brown.

4. Once cooked, you'll see that the mixture has risen a bit during cooking. This is where a little air is trapped in the base and you'll need to flatten it out: use the back of a spoon and apply gentle pressure to carefully flatten the mixture down from corner to corner. Then put this to one side while you make the caramel.

5. Make caramel. Weigh all the caramel ingredients straight into a medium-sized saucepan or high-edged medium frying pan. Put it on a medium heat and stir regularly. Once everything has melted (mainly the butter), set a timer for 10-12 minutes - you now need to stay with the saucepan throughout this time, gently mixing continuously to make sure the caramel doesn't burn and catch on the bottom or edges of the pan. The caramel will be getting really hot, so be super careful, and I would always recommend using the hob furthest away to avoid an accident.

6. As you reach the end of the 10 to 12 minutes on the timer, you'll notice that the caramel is more golden and has thickened and when you stir in the middle you should be able to see the bottom of the pan for a few seconds. If you're not sure if it's ready, keep cooking it for a few more minutes; it's much better to have slightly harder caramel than a runny one. Once ready, carefully pour the caramel from the pan straight over the shortbread base and level it out, being careful not to touch the caramel as it is ridiculously hot. I recommend using the back of a spoon.

7. Now place the tray in the fridge to cool down completely, allowing the caramel to harden up for at least 6 hours. If you're tempted to rush this part and go straight on to doing the chocolate, the heat from the caramel will spoil it and it won't look pretty...so my advice is that you just have to be patient!

Allergens in bold

Continued on next page >

Equipment

For the base

Tray, with high sides of at least 2cm high (1") and about 18cm wide x 27cm long (7" wide, 11" long)

Parchment paper

Electric whisk

Measuring spoons

Scales

For the caramel

High rimmed frying pan

Scales

Spatula

Whisk

For the chocolate topping

Small saucepan

Scales

Measuring jug

Mixing spoon

Small cup

Microwave

8. Make the ganache topping. Only make this once the caramel has completely set and is completely cool. In a small saucepan heat the cream until the steam just begins to rise from the surface, being careful not to overheat it. Add the chocolate cocoa nibs/small milk chocolate squares into the cream and allow them to sit for 30 seconds. Then starting from the middle, using a spoon, mix the chocolate nibs into the cream using circular motions, working from the middle to the outside and continue until the ganache is smooth and silky. If the chocolate hasn't fully melted, pop the pan back over a low heat for a minute or two, continuously stirring until the chocolate has fully melted into the cream.

9. Pour the ganache over the top of the caramel and smooth it right up to the edges, whilst keeping it in the tin. An optional finishing touch is to flick white melted chocolate over the top and create patterns, by gently running something sharp like a cocktail stick, pointy knife or fork through it. This is one of the most satisfying things to do.

10. Leave the tray to set in the fridge for about an hour before cutting in to your chosen portion size.

11. Store the millionaire shortbread squares airtight in the fridge for up to 7 days, or pop them in the freezer.

Top tips:

Be mindful of the size of the baking tin you're using. Look at suggested tin measurements for this recipe and measure the tin you have: if it's smaller or bigger, you might need to adjust the ingredients accordingly.

PS: at the time of writing this there is still an old video of the Millionaire shortbread being made at the coffee shop, by Ellie and I. To watch it, search "Nibsy's Millionaire shortbread" on YouTube for the full video.

Allergens in bold

Nutella & Banana Muffins

Not sure what makes these so addictive (maybe the oozing Nutella centre!) but if you've tried one before, you'll know what I mean! They are quite messy to make - you've been warned!

 9 to 12 chubby muffins   **30 mins**   **25-35 mins at 180°C**   **Yes**

Ingredients

- 240ml full-fat **milk** + add juice from 1 lemon
- 200g caster sugar
- 240g dairy-free spread or butter
- 5 medium **eggs**
- 240g gluten-free self raising flour
- 3 x teaspoon baking powder
- 1.5 x teaspoon xanthan gum
- 240g ground **almonds** (**nuts**)
- 1 x teaspoon salt
- 2 large or 3 small bananas, blended to a pulp
- 370g Nutella/chocolate spread (**nuts, milk, soya**)
- Optional: cocoa nibs and flaked **almonds** (**nuts**) or gluten-free **oats** to decorate

Equipment

Baking tray	Muffin cases	Scales

Measuring spoons	Electric whisk	Food processor

Large bowl	Spatula	Ice-cream scoop

Piping bag

Method

1. In a jug, measure the milk and add the lemon juice (you can use a different milk if you prefer) and leave to one side to develop for 10 minutes.

2. Preheat the oven to 180°C/350°F/gas mark 4. Line a 12-hole muffin tray with tulip/muffin cases (the ones that are bigger than the cupcake cases). If you can't get hold of these, I recommend you split this recipe into 20-24 cupcake sized portions, and use the classic cupcake style cases across 2 trays.

3. In a large bowl with a hand-held whisk, or using a cake mixer, combine the sugar and butter until light and fluffy. Add the eggs and mix until it looks a little curdled. Add the flour, baking powder, xanthan gum, ground almonds and salt. Thoroughly mix and slowly add the milk and lemon mixture. The batter should be thick and smooth. Then add the pulped bananas and mix everything together.

4. Now divide the batter into the muffin cases. If you want extra-large muffins, spread the batter across 9 cases. For the chocolate spread, we want to "inject" the muffins with about 40g of Nutella per muffin (and if making smaller muffins, reduce the amount of Nutella accordingly). You'll need a piping bag for this next bit. The chocolate spread might need melting a little in the microwave first (make sure there's no foil on the rim before putting it in the microwave; yes, I've made that mistake before!). Once soft, spoon it into a piping bag and cut a little hole at the end and squeeze the desired amount into the middle of each muffin.

5. Bake these in the pre-heated oven for 25-35 minutes at 180c (or less time if baking smaller sized ones). Once cooked, allow to cool for 10 minutes. To re-heat the cooked muffins so the chocolate goes gooey, pop them in the microwave for 30 seconds.

6. Once cooked, enjoy within 3 days. Store airtight at room temperature or freeze.

Top tips:

If you make a batch and don't plan on eating them all on the same day, you can pop the uncooked muffins in the freezer, in their tins (this keeps their shape while they freeze). And when you want one, simply pop the muffins in the oven and enjoy the smell of freshly baked muffins without the washing up!

Ilaria Marsigli (left)
Harriet Mummery (right)

Nutella Cake

Naturally gluten-free and light in texture but full of flavour, the added hazelnuts make this rather special. A favourite with kids and grown-ups, this first came along on what was apparently "National Nutella Day" some years back, and the bakers at the time, Harriet and Ilaria, created this "bad boy" as they'd say. It's nice slightly warmed up, in the microwave or as it comes at room temperature. A great little traveller too, which is why it was popular for take-aways and birthdays; a little bit of chocolate heaven, in a box!

 10 - 12 portions
1x 25cm (10") cake, single layer

 30 minutes

 40+ minutes at 180°C

 Yes

Ingredients

- 125g soft butter (**milk**)
- 1 pinch of salt
- 6 medium **eggs**, split (keeping egg yolks and egg whites separate)
- 1 x tablespoon hazelnut syrup (optional)
- 400g Nutella (**milk, soya, nuts**)
- 100g ground hazelnuts (**nuts**)
- 100g dark chocolate (**milk, soya**, depending on the brand you use)

Ganache topping

- 100ml double cream (**milk**)
- 1 x tablespoon hazelnut syrup (optional)
- 125g dark chocolate nibs (**milk, soya**, depending on the brand you use) or chocolate squares
- 4 x white chocolate squares (**soya, milk**)
- Handful of ground hazelnuts (**nuts**) to decorate

Equipment

 10" cake tin

 Scales

Measuring spoons

 Electric whisk

 Food processor

 Large bowl

 Small pan

 Spatula

Method

1. Preheat oven to 180°C/350°F/gas mark 4. Line the tin with a neat circle of parchment paper, placed in the base, so it goes as close to the edges as possible. Only line the base and not the sides for this one as lining the sides seems to affect the rise of the cake.

2. Using a large bowl and hand-held electric whisk or in a cake mixer, add the soft butter, salt, egg yolks (save the whites, you'll need them in a minute), hazelnut syrup and soft Nutella. Mix until well combined.

3. Grind the hazelnuts and leave them to one side.

4. Melt the dark chocolate in the microwave or in a glass bowl over a pan of water, until fully melted then add it, along with the ground hazelnuts to the rest of the ingredients and mix everything together again.

5. Using an electric hand-held whisk and a clean bowl, whisk the egg whites into stiff peaks. Pop a large dollop of the egg whites into the rest of the cake ingredients and gently mix; this will help to loosen the mixture.

6. By hand, gently fold in the remaining egg whites, a little at a time until all are combined. Make sure not to overmix the batter at this stage; just do the minimum to ensure the eggs are incorporated whilst not knocking too much air out of them, and then pour the mixture into the cake tin.

7. Bake for 35 to 40 minutes. Check with a skewer or sharp knife before taking it out. It might need a little longer. Once baked, leave to cool and then transfer on to a plate, ready to be covered in chocolate!

8. Make the ganache. Make this once the cake has cooled down and is ready to be iced. In a small saucepan heat the cream and syrup until the steam just begins to rise from the surface, being careful not to overheat it. Add the chocolate cocoa nibs/small chocolate squares into the cream and allow them to sit for 30 seconds. Then starting from the middle, using a spoon, mix the chocolate into the cream using circular motions, working from the middle to the outside and continue until the ganache is smooth and silky. If the chocolate hasn't fully melted, pop the pan back over a low heat for a minute or two, continuously stirring until the chocolate has fully melted into the cream.

9. Pour the ganache over the top of the cooled cake and smooth it over right up to the edges. An optional finishing touch is to flick white melted chocolate over the cake. And to create patterns, gently run something sharp like a fork through it. Or you can just add more hazelnuts, either whole or blended ones along with fruit etc.

10. If you'd like the cake re-heated, each slice just needs a flash in the microwave, for about 15 to 20 seconds. Store airtight in the fridge for up to 4 days, or freeze.

Orange & Almond Cake

This "upside-down" cake can easily be confused for a polenta cake, but this one is made with ground almonds and contains no polenta whatsoever. It does mean it's a bit pricier to make but there's nothing else quite like the freshness and simplicity of this cake. This was first made at the coffee shop by the talented Ilaria who was the first baker I ever employed, and it's made many people happy over the years. And now, you can make it at home!

 10 - 12 portions
1x 25cm (10") cake

 40 mins

 50 mins - 1 hour at 170°C

 Yes

Ingredients

- 415g boiled oranges; it's about 4 large oranges which must be weighed after being boiled to the weight of exactly 415g.
- 1 orange for decorating
- 350g ground **almonds** (**nuts**)
- 300g caster sugar
- 3 x teaspoon baking powder
- 6 medium **eggs**
- Small handful **almonds** (**nuts**) and pumpkin seeds to decorate

Orange glaze

- 100ml orange juice
- 100g caster sugar

Equipment

10" cake tin	Parchment paper	Scales
Measuring spoons	Electric whisk	Food processor
Large bowl	Small pan	Spatula

Method

1. Put the oranges in a large pan of boiling water and boil them on a medium to low heat for 30 minutes, then drain. This water is really good for clearing the pipes in your kitchen sink!

2. Preheat the oven to 170°C/325°F/gas mark 3. Grease your tin with a tiny bit of sunflower or vegetable oil. Cut a piece of parchment paper to sit inside the base of the tin and cut a separate strip to go around the inside of the cake tin. The reason the parchment paper is so important with this one is because the cake is so dense, and the cooking time is long, so it's important the cake is well protected.

3. Slice the decorating orange as thinly as possible and place the slices around the bottom of the lined cake tin and sprinkle almond flakes and pumpkin or sunflower seeds over them.

4. In a large bowl or cake mixer, mix together the ground almonds, sugar and baking powder and then add the eggs and mix everything together.

5. Once the oranges have finished boiling for 30 minutes, chop them into chunks (to help them blend better) and put them in a food processor and blend them to a smooth pulp. Pour the blended oranges into the bowl and mix vigorously to get some air into the mixture, to help the cake rise a bit more.

6. Spoon the mixture into the cake tin and bake for about 50 minutes to 1 hour. It's a good idea to check the cake half way through cooking in case it needs to be rotated 180 degrees in the oven for an even bake. Once the cake looks ready, using a skewer or knife, check that the centre is cooked. If in doubt, cook another 5 minutes and keep checking. Once cooked, the cake should feel firm but spongy and golden in colour.

7. Once cool, tip out the cake, upside down and place it on a plate or board and carefully remove the parchment paper to reveal the cake.

8. Glaze. This is to simply add a little sheen to the top of the cake. In a small saucepan mix the orange juice and caster sugar together. Simmer until reduced and thicker, stirring occasionally; this should take about 30 minutes. Drizzle a small amount on the top of the cake with a pastry brush or the back of a spoon. Store the leftover glaze in the fridge.

9. Store airtight in the fridge for up to 4 days, or freeze.

Allergens in bold

Pastry
Can also be dairy free too

In the autumn of 2013, my husband Jon surprised me with a course he'd booked me to go on. It was a day of learning how to make pastry and bread with Adriana Rabinovich at a Miele demonstration centre near Oxford. I knew I needed to gain some confidence if I was seriously going to open a gluten-free coffee shop instead of returning to my office job after maternity leave ended. But it was early days and I'd not yet even put pen to paper, I just spent my days baking, trying to learn. I drove there, not knowing what to expect. The course was incredible, and Adriana shared so much passion for the recipes and methods she came up with and wanted to make sure we all 'got it'. I think she said the pastry took her about 10 years to master, a proper labour of love and determination, as she tried to find alternative solutions to everyday pleasures that her daughter could no longer eat after becoming intolerant to gluten.

Adriana supported me when the shop opened by not only believing in it, but allowing us to use her pastry recipe. So I passed on the knowledge to the bakers and over the years we have found ways to build in shortcuts, without compromising the final result. It's got Adriana's approval! It is consistently quick, reliable and possibly the best gluten-free pastry you will ever taste. So to be able to share this with you is a huge gift from Adriana. It opens up so many possibilities. And you can make the pastry dairy-free too. To help, there is a video where I show you how to make it. To view it on YouTube, search for Nibsy's YouTube channel.

 1 batch produces:
1 x 25cm (10") quiche flan dish,
or 10 x 10cm (4") tins,
or 18 cupcake sized tins

 10 minutes

 15-20 mins at 190°C (depending on the size of the tins)

 Yes

Ingredients

- 235g gluten-free plain flour (I recommend Doves Farm)
- 125g **butter** frozen into chunks (or vegan butter block by FLORA)
- 1 x teaspoon salt
- 1 medium **egg** (from the fridge)
- 2 x tablespoon ice cold water if using butter. If making it dairy-free just 1 x tablespoon

Equipment

Having a Magimix style food processor is ESSENTIAL for making the pastry. It helps limit hand contact with the pastry which would otherwise make the pastry warm and therefore difficult to work with.

Scales Measuring spoons Rolling pin

Parchment paper Clingfilm Small bowl

Jug of ice water Palette knife Food processor

Notes:

If you're reading this for the first time and want to make the pastry right away, you will first need to put 125g frozen butter, cut into about 6 little chunks in the freezer for at least 6 hours. The pastry is much harder to work with if the butter is only cold from the fridge – It must be frozen.

If you're making pastry for a sweet item, please still add the salt – it's a vital ingredient to help create a crumbly texture

Method

1. There are two things that are critical to making the pastry a success:

   A) Speed (because heat is the enemy here) and confidence, which of course only comes after practice. It may feel hard at first, but like many things when you've practised, it will get much easier, and your confidence will help you work quickly, which in turn helps to create beautiful pastry.

   B) Using frozen butter, ice cold water, cold egg(s) from the fridge and use a food processor.

   Note: I have done a video for you, which is on YouTube Video and can be found by searching for Nibsy's Youtube channel. The recipe is quite wordy so this allows you to see all the steps in action, and how easy they are.

2. Cut 125g of butter into about 6 pieces and freeze it for 6 hours or more. It must be frozen when you come to use it. And put the egg(s) you'll be using in the fridge.

3. Once the butter is frozen you can start. Preheat the oven to 190C/350F/gas mark 5. Put a teaspoon of salt and 235g gluten-free plain flour by Doves farm into the food processor, along with the chunks of frozen butter.

4. Whizz the machine on full power until it resembles fine sand. To check it, lift the lid and carefully touch the mixture to see if it feels like the butter is truly broken down, whilst not being over mixed at this stage, or it will get greasy and overworked.

5. Now add to the food processor: 1 cold egg along with either 1 tablespoon of the iced water if using dairy-free butter or 2 tablespoons ice cold water when using cow's butter.

6. On full power, blitz it for about a minute. You will probably need to stop it once or twice as you'll notice the bottom rim of the food processor might gather mixture that's not being picked up by the blades. To unstick this mixture, use a palette knife and just quickly scrape away the sides and loosen it. Blitz again, at full speed, with your eyes on the pastry at all times; it should start to come together like a dough ball. As soon as it comes together, stop whizzing it: it's ready to be used.

7. Carefully take the shaggy pastry ball out, along with any loose bits and tip it on to the worksurface. Quickly bring the dough together in a ball as quickly as possible to avoid overheating it with your hands. Now you have a rough ball, lift it up to shoulder height (whilst still being aware of minimizing how much heat it gets from your hands) and drop it down onto the worktop and repeat this 20 times, quickly. This is an important stage as it helps reduce the cracks in the pastry once cooked. The pastry can either be rolled now (read on) or wrapped in clingfilm and kept in the fridge for up to 4 days or in the freezer.

8. To fill a large flan dish/pastry case: You may want to line the large baking dish first (especially if making a quiche or a dish that has a wet filling, to prevent it leaking through any possible gaps). To line the tin, use screwed up parchment paper which you then unscrew and push into the dish, making sure all the inner edges of the tin are well taken care of. Park to one side.

9. Roll the pastry. Place a large sheet of parchment paper on to your worktop, with a light sprinkle of the gluten-free flour. Place the pastry ball in the centre of the parchment paper with another little sprinkling of flour on the top. Grab a large sheet of clingfilm and lay it over the pastry ball. Using a rolling pin, give the pastry a good few 'slams' as to flatten it out a bit before rolling.

10. Keep the large sheet of clingfilm over the top and roll over it until you have a large circle of pastry that's about 35cm (14") wide and 2-3mm (3/4-1") thick. Make sure the thickness is the same throughout. If you think it needs re-rolling better, working as quickly as you can (as the pastry will be warming up) take away the cling, gather it back into a shaggy ball, place it back on the parchment paper, put the cling-film over the top and repeat.

11. Now turn back to the pastry ball. Keep the pastry in-between the layer of parchment and clingfilm, but flip it over, so you now have the parchment side facing up and the cling-film side is touching the worktop. If it's showing lots of crinkles, soften them out using a rolling pin. Now gently peel away the parchment paper. Place one hand and forearm underneath the pastry, and flip it over and into the large tin. The cling film will now be facing up and the pastry is underneath, draped over the tin. The pastry has no "stretch" due to there not being any gluten. So the pastry can't be forced into the sides of the tin or it will simply crack more than usual during cooking: You therefore need to gently lift and delicately feed the pastry into the sides, working your way around the rim of the tin up to the top of the sides. Any overhanging pastry can be trimmed away, using your hands.

12. Once the pastry in in place, very gently peel away the clingfilm, being careful not to lift the pastry up with it. If there are any areas of the pastry that need a bit of 'patching up' and filling in, use a little bit of the leftover pastry like 'Polyfilla' to fill in the areas that need attention.

13. This now goes into the oven at 190°C for 15-20 minutes, until golden.

14. To roll smaller cases you'll need cake cutters. Once you've rolled the pastry to 2-3mm thick, gently peel away the clingfilm. Using your chosen cutter, place and cut out the shapes, still working quickly as the pastry becomes harder to work with the warmer it gets. Using a palette knife or flat serving tool, place it under the shape and lift it off from the parchment paper and place it over the tin it's going to be cooked in. You'll need to gently coach the shapes into the tins, and once ready, cook in a pre-heated oven at 190°C for about 15 minutes or more, until golden.

15. Fill the pastry with delicious flavours. From quiches to tarts, see each recipe for full details.

16. Storing the pastry if making it in advance. The raw pastry ball lasts up to 4 days when kept airtight in the fridge or can be frozen too. When rolling the raw pastry, it's best to take it straight from the fridge. If it gets too warm and therefore difficult to handle, pop it back in the fridge until it's cold enough to work with again.

Popcorn Bars

These are really easy to make and you can vary them to your liking by using a different type of chocolate and caramel; in this recipe everything is vegan. You may want to add nuts and other delights to this too. Just bear in mind it needs an hour to "set" in the freezer before you can cut into it and enjoy. The idea for these came from my cousin and very close friend, Lorena. She gave me an interesting looking gluten-free bar from one of the high street coffee chains that was made with popcorn and caramel and tasted really good. And so it inspired me to make this version.

 8 portions
1 rectangular tin: 27cm (10.5") x 18cm (7") and 2.5cm (1") deep

 40 minutes +
1 hour in the freezer

 Yes

Ingredients

For the caramel

- ½ can of coconut milk (so 200ml)
- 75g light brown sugar
- ½ x teaspoon vanilla essence
- 1 x teaspoon cracked salt

For the bars

- 240g dairy-free white chocolate (may contain **soya**)
- 50g popcorn (sweet, salty or mixture)
- 60g gluten-free crispy rice cereals
- 40g cranberries
- 40g raisins

For the topping

- 30g melted dark, dairy-free chocolate (may contain **soya**)
- Sprinkling of coconut flakes

Equipment

Baking tray

Parchment paper

Rolling pin

Scales

Measuring spoons

Saucepan

Large bowl

Method

1. First, make the caramel, which will take 25 minutes. Shake the coconut milk before opening and pour half the can into a pan with the brown sugar and vanilla essence. Regularly stir it on a medium heat for 25 minutes. The caramel won't be very thick but it's used for drizzling on top of the popcorn bars, so it doesn't need to be firm. Once the caramel is ready, stir in the salt and leave it to one side while you prepare the popcorn bars.

2. Line the tin with parchment paper so it comes up all four sides. Gently melt the white chocolate in the microwave or in a small bowl over simmering water in a pan, making sure the water doesn't touch the bowl.

3. In a large bowl mix the popcorn, gluten-free crispy rice cereals, raisins and cranberries and once melted, mix in the white chocolate. There isn't much chocolate in this recipe so it needs to be well mixed to get it distributed throughout.

4. Pour the mixture into the tin. It should initially look like there is a bit too much but it should eventually all fit (unless your tin is much smaller). Spread the mixture evenly across the lined tray. To help flatten and condense the mixture, to make more solid units, cut a large sheet of parchment paper and place it over the top. Using a rolling pin, bash, press and roll the mixture firmly into the baking tin.

5. Once the mixture is looking satisfyingly flattened, drizzle the caramel over it. Melt the dark chocolate in the microwave and flick this over the top followed by the coconut flakes.

6. It's now ready to be placed in the freezer for 1 hour to set. Once cool, remove the tray from the freezer and cut the slab into little bars while it's still frozen as it's much easier when hard and will create well-defined edges. It's a good idea to then individually wrap these and then store the bars in the fridge or even in the freezer as they can pretty much be eaten straight from the freezer!

7. Store airtight and in the fridge or freezer.

Allergens in bold

Ellie Walker - 2020

Rocky Road

I never really liked Rocky Road. Always found them too sweet and sugary. One day, one of the longest serving bakers at the coffee shop, Ellie (pictured), said she could make a really tasty and grown-up vegan Rocky Road. She wasn't wrong! So if you want to recreate the exact same Rocky Roads as we did, it's all about making sure to use good quality ingredients. Thank you Ellie for making lots of people very happy with these little treats.

 10 portions
1x 20cm (8") square tin

 30 minutes

 Yes

Ingredients

- 45g maple syrup
- 125g dairy-free spread
- 300g vegan dark chocolate, ideally 53% cocoa solids (may contain **soya**)
- 200g gluten-free, dairy-free digestive biscuits (may contain gluten-free **oats**)
- 100g vegan marshmallows (a brand called Mallows are very good and are available in Holland and Barrett)
- Icing sugar for dusting (optional)

Equipment

20cm square tin   Parchment paper   Saucepan

Glass bowl   Spatula   Mixing spoon

Method

1. Line a square tin with parchment paper, allowing the paper to come up and over the top of the tin; it helps to lift the Rocky Road out of the tin later.

2. Pop a saucepan of water on medium heat on the hob, and in a large glass or metal bowl weigh in the maple syrup, dairy-free spread and chocolate. Place the bowl over the saucepan, making sure the water doesn't touch the bowl, and melt the ingredients together, stirring regularly.

3. Meanwhile, in separate bowl, weigh and break up the biscuits whilst still leaving chunky bits. If the marshmallows are large ones, you may want to cut them in half and then add these in the bowl with the biscuits.

4. Once the chocolate mixture has melted and looks glossy, take it off the heat and add the broken biscuits and marshmallows to it and mix until everything is well combined.

5. Pour the mixture into the tin, scraping down the sides with a spatula to get every last bit in there. Spread the mixture evenly across the tin and into the corners. Put it in the fridge to set until firm; for at least 4 hours.

6. Once the slab has fully hardened up, it's ready to be cut into your chosen size followed by a sprinkle of icing sugar, to finish them off nicely.

7. Keep them airtight and in the fridge for up to 7 days, or freeze.

Allergens in bold

Scones (vegan)

This recipe is based on the classic fluffy scone recipe and has been adapted so more people could enjoy them. These vegan versions are just as good as the classic ones and I sometimes find it hard to tell the difference between them. There is a great vegan butter called FLORA Plant Butter. It's available at many of the large supermarkets and it's totally worthwhile getting your hands on it for making these scones. But if you can't source this, you can use vegan spread instead.

I'd never made as many of these as I did during January 2021 when the UK was in lockdown and we wanted to celebrate 'Veganuary' but were temporally closed. My husband, Jon, and I decided to make and deliver vegan treat boxes, which included these beauties. Due to the surprise volume of orders we had, I'd be up extra early most mornings and in the kitchen baking and by late morning Jon would arrive to help box them all up ready to load into the back of car and deliver in and around Reading and beyond on those cold winter days. Great memories.

8 scones	20 minutes	16 - 20 minutes at 180°C	Yes

Ingredients

Wet

- 150ml **soya** milk
- 150ml double **soya** cream (Alpro is great)
- 2.5 x teaspoon apple cider vinegar
- 120g aquafaba (water from tinned chickpeas)

Dry

- 100g vegan butter (ideally FLORA block)
- 500g gluten-free self-raising flour
- 50g sugar
- 2 x teaspoon baking powder
- 1 x teaspoon xanthan gum
- 1 x teaspoon salt

Equipment

Large bowl

Scales

Measuring spoons

Electric whisk

Flat baking tray

Ice-cream scoop

Sieve

Method

1. Pre-heat the oven to 180°C/350°F/gas mark 4 and line a large baking tray with parchment paper.

2. In a jug, combine all the wet ingredients and leave them to one side to 'develop' for 10 minutes.

3. Using an electric hand-held whisk or cake mixer, add the softened vegan butter to a large bowl and sieve over half of the flour (sieving the flour results in fluffier scones). Mix until it's crumbly. Then sieve the rest of the flour and add the sugar, baking powder, xanthan gum and salt and mix it all together.

4. Gently pour the wet ingredients in with the dry ingredients and thoroughly mix them together until you have a smooth and fairly wet looking batter. Using an ice cream scoop or spoon, pop 2 dollops on top of one another, straight onto the lined baking tray, leaving at least 5cm gaps between the scones, so they have room to expand in the oven.

5. Bake for 16 minutes, turning the tray around halfway through the bake to ensure they are evenly cooked. Depending on your oven, they may need a little longer.

6. Allow to cool for about 10 minutes and enjoy. To reheat, pop them in the microwave for 20 seconds or so.

7. Enjoy within 2 days and store airtight and at room temperature or freeze.

Allergens in bold

STICKY
TOFFEE
PUD

110

Sticky Toffee Pudding

Before going gluten-free, this was my pudding of choice when eating out. I used to work as a waitress in a country pub called The Crown, in Playhatch, and they made a splendid sticky toffee pudding; I'd recommend it to customers and my manager and the pastry chef would often comment on how many more they'd sell on the shifts I worked. After changing to a gluten-free diet and feeling a million times better for it, I'd still miss eating this pudding, a lot.

When the idea of running my own business was still a pipe dream, it was one of the recipes I played around with at home. I'd try it out on friends and family and they'd say there was no compromise on texture and flavour, despite it being gluten-free and dairy-free. It's a proper comforting, light and fluffy recipe and although it didn't get made at the coffee shop very often, I feel it belongs in this book! I hope you enjoy making it!

6 portions 1 x 20cm (8") square tin or similar size	**40 minutes**	**35 - 45 minutes at 170°C**	❄ **Yes**

Ingredients

- 225g whole pitted dates or ready chopped
- 175ml boiling water
- 140g soft brown sugar
- 85g dairy-free spread or vegan butter block and extra for greasing
- 2 large **eggs**
- 1 x teaspoon vanilla extract
- 175g gluten-free self-raising flour
- 1 x teaspoon bicarbonate of soda
- 125ml **soya** milk

Toffee Sauce

- 170g light brown muscovado sugar
- 55g dairy-free spread or vegan butter block
- 275ml dairy-free cream, such as **soya** cream

Method

1. Pre-heat oven to 170°C/325°F/gas mark 3 and line your baking tray with parchment paper.

2. Put pitted dates in bowl and cover with 175ml boiling water. Leave them to rest for 30 minutes, then blend them in a food processor until smooth, along with any of the water that has not been absorbed.

3. Meanwhile, using an electric or manual whisk, beat the sugar and dairy-free spread together until light and creamy. Add the eggs and vanilla extract and mix everything again. Then, thoroughly mix in the flour and bicarbonate of soda. Finally, add the soya milk and the blended dates to the rest of the batter. It will look a little curdled - that's normal!

4. Spoon mixture into the baking tin and cook for 35-40 minutes.

5. Make toffee sauce. Put the sugar and dairy-free spread with half the soya cream into a saucepan and bring to the boil on a medium heat, stirring at all times until the sugar has dissolved. This will only take a few minutes.

6. Stir in the remaining cream and then take it off the heat.

7. Once the sticky toffee pudding has cooled down, take it out of the tin and cut into portions and drizzle over the toffee sauce. To re-heat, use a microwave.

8. Store airtight and in the fridge for up to 4 days, or freeze.

Equipment

8" square baking tray

Parchment paper

Scales

Measuring spoons

Hand whisk

Spatula

Large bowl

Small bowl

Vegan Chocolate Crunch Bars

I literally* dreamt this one up. I had a craving for something indulgent, nutty, slightly crunchy and not too sweet. To my astonishment the first attempt was 'the one' that fulfilled this. It's the one sweet item that my mum asks me to bring when I visit her. And she doesn't have a sweet tooth. Personally, I think these taste great with a quality glass of red wine.
*(sorry Dad, I know you don't like the loose use of this word!)

 10 bars
1 x 20cm (8") square tin   **20 minutes**   **4 hours in the fridge**   **Yes**

Ingredients

Wet

- 150g dairy-free soft spread
- 75g coconut oil, melted
- 3 x tablespoons **almond** butter (**nuts**)
- 75g maple syrup
- 1 x pinch of salt
- ½ x teaspoon vanilla essence
- 300g 70% dark, vegan chocolate (may contain **soya**)

Dry

- 75g gluten-free crispy rice cereals
- 75g gluten-free corn flakes

Topping

- 25g cranberries
- 25g **almond** flakes (**nuts**)
- 25g raisins
- 15g pumpkin seeds

Equipment

8" square tin	Parchment paper	Saucepan

Scales	Large bowl	Measuring spoons

Method

1. Neatly line the square tin with parchment paper with the paper coming up and over the sides. You'll need to pull on this paper later in order to get the vegan crunch out of the tin, with ease.

2. Weigh all the 'wet' ingredients along with the chocolate (which you'll need to break into little pieces unless you're using cocoa nibs) into a large glass or metal bowl. Place the bowl over a saucepan of hot water on a low heat, making sure the hot water doesn't touch the bowl.

3. Slowly melt all the ingredients together, stirring regularly until it all looks glossy. Everything will melt beautifully, apart from the almond butter which has a different kind of texture. Just try and get it mixed in as best you can!

4. Take the bowl off the heat and add the corn flakes and crispy rice cereals into the chocolate mixture and make sure it's all really well mixed in. Once everything is well incorporated and all the cereals are covered in chocolate etc spoon it into the tin and press down firmly using the back of a spoon to ensure the mixture is level, flat and well packed in, all the way into the corners.

5. Finally, sprinkle the slab with seeds, nuts and berries and press these down gently so that they stick and hold a bit better once it's ready to be cut. It will now need to go in the fridge for at least 4 hours, to harden up before cutting.

6. Once the slab has gone hard from being in the fridge, it can be cut. Just pull the slab out of the tin using the excess parchment paper and place it on a chopping board and cut to your desired size.

7. Store these bars in the fridge for up to 7 days and keep them airtight to retain freshness. Also suitable for freezing.

115

Thanks & Acknowledgements

This book has not been put together through a publisher, which is probably why it took me a lot longer than I anticipated!

A huge thank you to my husband Jon for being so supportive, kind (and tolerant of me) and I wouldn't have had the confidence to do much without you.

Thanks to my mum, Cathy Stoker, for bringing me up to believe the sky's the limit and always being there. My best friend and life companion.

A big cheers to my dad, David Stoker, for all the proof-reading you had to do on this, for being a legend and for always being encouraging.

Big thanks to Adriana Rabinovich for all the encouragement and insight during the earlier stages of getting this project off the ground.

Thank you Hilary Scott - when I hit a wall with the final stages of recipe proof-reading and you did all the important polishing up that was needed.

Thank you Elizabeth Kenny for taking such beautiful photos of me as well as the bakewell photos. And thank you Melissa Wood for doing my make-up and making me feel amazing.

Although I took all the food photos myself (on the iPhone), I'd like to thank Sue Archer who kindly gave me a quick crash course session in food photography in 2020.

Huge thanks to Brad and Dean and the team at Seen In Design for all the work you did creating this book and making it real!

Thank you to my friends. In particular my cousin, Lorena Gushlow, for listening to me when I was finding things especially hard and for all the words of wisdom. Thank you Leigh-Anne Strong for all the laughs and never doubting me.

Thank you to Richard Ingham for creating all the branding of my dreams in 2014 and for helping over the years with your exceptional talent.

I couldn't have done much without the help of Natasha Pierse – a truly amazing childminder. Thank you so much.

Past team members

Thanks to all the amazing front of house and baking team who've been employed at some point, with well over 50 of you. Had it not been for your involvement in making Nibsy's a success, it's unlikely I'd have put this book together. I'd like to specifically mention a few people:

From the baking team (in the order in which they joined):

Ilaria Marsigli – The brains behind some of the best recipes in here. Anything you did, you turned it to gold and what a positive impact you had during those crucial first 18 months.

Harriet Mummery who worked incredibly efficiently in our little kitchen, always organised and one step ahead, finding ways to make things work better.

Eleanor Walker for making everything taste super and being effortlessly productive and a great baking companion.

Céline Lee for sharing your gift and love of vegan baking and sharing your rare talent.

From the front of house team, those I'd especially like to thank are (in the order in which they joined):

Rachel Knight for being the first ever Barista I employed and helping me find my feet in those early days and for being so patient with me.

Rachel McCourt for all the fun and laughs, and the hard work you put in, as well as seeing the value in what I was trying to achieve.

Libby Penny for being the loveliest young lady with everyone, a true gem.

Leah Lemm-Surruya for helping with ideas and making me laugh when things got stressful.

Anna Chalker (who also helped in the kitchen) for all the attention to detail and passion for gluten-free food and being a total advocate for the business.

Esther Hanley-Clarke for being pure class in every way.

Jess Gibson for superb communication and holding everything together on till, on the busiest shifts of the week.

Billie-Mae Beilby (who also helped in the kitchen) for always being calm, efficient and a brilliant team member.

Natalie Webb for being the most kind, professional and meticulous person I've ever had the pleasure of working with, and always taking pride in your work.

Rebecca Parsons for having a heart of gold and being the food station and fridge-cleaning queen.

Thank you so much Laura Tilley (who also helped in the kitchen) for being so conscientious and an all-round brilliant multi-tasker.

And a big thank you to everyone else involved who I've not mentioned here.

You

And finally, thank you to all the people who would ask when the book would be ready. Had it not been for those lovely nudges, I may have never finished it!

Nibsy's Gluten-Free Recipes
Naomi Lowe
2021

info@nibsys.com
www.nibsys.com
Instagram: @nibsysgf
Facebook: Gluten-free Nibsy
Twitter: @nibsysgf

Design & Typeset by Seen In Design
(www.seenindesign.com)
Photography by Naomi Lowe
Photography of front and rear cover, bakewells
and portraits of Naomi by Elizabeth Kenny
(www.lizkennyphotography.co.uk)

ISBN 978-1-3999-1152-8